# THE RHETORIC OF BLACK POWER

*Under the Advisory Editorship of J. Jeffery Auer*

# THE RHETORIC OF BLACK POWER

*Robert L. Scott*   *University of Minnesota*

*Wayne Brockriede*   *University of Colorado*

GREENWOOD PRESS, PUBLISHERS
WESTPORT, CONNECTICUT

**Library of Congress Cataloging in Publication Data**

Scott, Robert Lee, 1928-    comp.
   The rhetoric of Black power.

    Reprint of the ed. published by Harper & Row, New York.
    Bibliography:  p.
    1.  Black power--United States--Addresses, essays,
lectures.  2.  Afro-Americans--Psychology--Addresses,
essays, lectures.  I.  Brockriede, Wayne, joint comp.
II.  Title.
[E185.615.S34 1979]        301.45'19'6073      78-31755
ISBN 0-313-20973-1

First J. & J. Harper edition 1969.

Reprinted with the permission of Harper & Row, Publishers, Inc.

Reprinted in 1979 by Greenwood Press, Inc.
51 Riverside Avenue, Westport, CT 06880

Printed in the United States of America

10  9  8  7  6  5  4  3  2  1

# CONTENTS

# *Preface*

Black Power is a revolutionary force in American life. Whatever may be the resolution of the demands and denials now spinning about the term, what it means to be an American can never again be quite the same. The results of revolutions are never what even the most clear-eyed observers predict and certainly never what any of the most deeply involved participants want. If the forces which make history are more than anyone can understand or control, they are pervasive. Man must struggle to understand and to influence. To do less than struggle with the issues of one's own lifetime is to be less than fully human.

Both advantages and disadvantages result from using radically contemporary materials for educational purposes. The involved participant of contemporary affairs will have difficulty in seeing them in any sort of perspective. The very idea of perspective suggests a standing apart, a quiescence that Black Power simply will not permit. But education is not something entirely abstracted from one's important and immediate feelings. Each person's education must include an immediate relevance of what he knows to his very existence. Plunging into the study of issues like those surrounding Black Power is vital; it should not be delayed in the name of objectivity, reliability, academic respectability, or any other god-term of institutionalized education.

The pressures growing out of Black Power are not apt to be transmuted quickly into a calm reinforcement of the old American Way. If the power of the American Way is its ability to adapt itself to change, Black Power may give that American power one of its more severe trials. Will the inevitable modifications strengthen or weaken its institutions? Black Power's radical confrontation with the established power in this country reveals strong strains of hypocrisy in the system. The Establishment may be able to purge these tendencies. In rage at the revelation, eager for a righteous self-justification, it may contort democratic institutions into Orwellian molds long before 1984. It has the economic and political power to buy off or rub out those who denounce things-as-they-are. It also has the economic and political power and, it is hoped, strong enough democratic traditions to work out accommodations that will not be uneasy compromises but substantial solutions to the social ills of which Black Power is symptomatic.

Black Power, no matter what shapes it assumes in the next few years, will remain vital as one starting point for the study of the American ethos which is now developing and which will dominate lives for the last quarter of the twentieth century.

RLS
WB

*Minneapolis and Boulder*

# THE RHETORIC OF BLACK POWER

# CHAPTER ONE

## An Introduction to the Rhetoric of Black Power

Traditionally, rhetoric has been the study of verbal persuasion. Most men, living in communities with other men, find that satisfying their needs and desires entails inducing the cooperation of others. All animals have patterns of behavior with which to communicate with their kind, but these patterns are highly fixed and ritualistic, such as the courtship dances of geese or the shrill cries that indicate the occupation of territory by a jaguar. Although a good deal of man's symbolic behavior is ritualistic, his use of language is capable of a high degree of conscious manipulation that enables him to create fresh meanings and to communicate the symbols of these meanings to his fellows more or less efficiently.

Although no more important than the ordinary ritualistic communicative interchanges scarcely thought of as having rhetorical impact, the large, purposive actions we call speeches, essays, pamphlets, discussions, debates, and so forth are verbal patternings clearly regarded as rhetorical. Often these verbalizations are formed into rather elaborate campaigns on behalf of some point of view or product. At other times they are scattered, and anyone who senses them must discover the relationships.

The alert reader who studies the struggle for civil rights for black Americans, out of which the cry for Black Power has come, may wonder about our tendency to feature the verbal. After all, the strike and protest march, the sit-in and the vigil of silent prayer are indelibly identified with what came to be called in the late 1950s and early 1960s The Movement. These are nonverbal rhetorical thrusts designed to influence the behavior of others in ways that would be conducive finally to the ends sought by those who struck, protested, sat, and prayed. Such people have acted out in starkly dramatic terms the case against what had become by desire and design or by acquiescence American institutions. The media, especially television, gave these symbolic actions wide currency.

In addition to nonverbal actions that have rhetorical impact, such nonverbal cues as the gestures and tone of voice a speaker employs also affect how receivers respond to the verbal discourse. The color of the ink and the quality of the paper may be similar nonverbal cues that a pamphleteer may attend to carefully or perpetrate carelessly. All these cues can influence response.

As Leonard Doob pointed out in the introduction to his pioneering book on propaganda thirty years ago, the band and the flag are as much a part of the rally as are the speeches. Doob tends to treat nonverbal elements as reinforcing the verbal message. From another point of view, they seem to summarize: They may be the simplest symbolic embodiments of the complex store of feelings and meanings that the more or less organized body of believers seems to bring to bear on the beliefs and actions of others.

In considering the rhetoric of Black Power, we shall concentrate on the verbal. We can explain, if not justify, the emphasis. An introduction must start somewhere and must omit something. The words are too apparent and too important to omit. Further, an understanding of the nonverbal usually presupposes an understanding of the verbal. Finally, a critic has much more difficulty in giving a decent account of nonverbal elements than of verbal, especially when the analysis is communicated on a printed page.

The concept of rhetoric invites a fundamental ambiguity in focusing on verbal discourse. At times it seems to refer to the means of persuasion, as contrasted with specific ends a persuader may seek and with particular materials he may use. From this point of view, the rhetoric of Black Power would include verbal patternings that could be abstracted from the stuff of the arguments and shared with arguments on other subjects far different. For example, a speaker may feel the need to identify his interest with those of a group of listeners. A critic may discover how the speaker goes about accomplishing this task and notice that his means of identifying resemble those of other speakers who deal with quite different goals and materials. Noticing how speakers and writers proceed on a multitude of occasions may give rise to a more or less coherent body of doctrine which can be referred to as a rhetoric. Such procedures, together with the testimony of generations of speakers and writers as to how they do go about their tasks, have formed a rather sizeable body of rhetorical tradition.

At other times, rather than referring to these subject-free means which have been observed to be useful in persuasion, rhetoric refers to the particular arguments on a subject and to the special interaction of people in a situation. From this point of view, the rhetoric of Black Power would include the tendencies to shape lines of argument favorable or unfavorable to that subject and to influence kinds of interpersonal relationships. For example, a Black Power advocate might argue that the assassination of Malcolm X was the result of a racist conspiracy. If a critic found that charges of conspiracy were common in Black Power rhetoric, or in the rhetoric of some advocate of Black Power, he might be interested in how the arguments on that theme seem to typify the discourse with which he is confronted.

Both concepts of rhetoric have some utility. The traditions will provide useful beginnings in looking at a body of discourse for the unique patterns it may contain. On the other hand, focusing on the unique substance of any controversy will enable a critic to see rhetoric as a dynamic set of tendencies, not as dogmatic prescriptions. Too often, unhappily, rhetoric has been nothing but the latter. In examining the rhetoric of Black Power we shall be dominated by the view of rhetoric as patterns of argument and human interaction that tend to grow out of the situations in which Black Power is urged and denounced.

Seeing rhetoric as situational is to guard against some common dangers. Critics are too prone to see persons involved in persuasion as grand actors without taking due account of the scenes in which they act. Clearly, the advocate of Black Power (or his opponent) is the product of persuasive forces that have worked on him. Stokely Carmichael, for example, although a young man, spent several years intensely organizing and carrying out projects carefully adhering to the ideals that gave the Student Nonviolent Coordinating Committee its name, a name that in many ears sounds today like high irony. The successes and failures of his work modified him until he became the instrument of a cry with a different import than "We Shall Overcome."

Just as Stokely Carmichael has tried to shape the responses of those about him, the audiences that he has addressed have had shaping influences on him. He has demanded; but they have demanded, too. The increasing shrillness of his recommendations, and those of H. Rap Brown, interpreted by many observers as inciting violence, may well have been shaped more by audiences' responses than by their own attempts to modify tendencies to respond. A speaker chooses his audiences and is chosen or rejected by them; but on neither side are the consciousness and control perfect. One involved can only recognize the potentialities of the circumstances within which he must act, or refuse to act, and utilize these potentialities as well as he can. Another person, at the same time or at a different time, might view the potentialities quite differently; indeed, for him they might be quite different.

Speaker and audience influence each other within a social context. For many black Americans the situation is the terribly frustrating one of working for goals of equal opportunity in a country predominantly white. Walls of ignorance prove as debilitating to their efforts as open hatred and savage repression. What seem to some to be genuine signs of progress in civil rights legislation are to others tokens devoid of meaning. The U.S. Commission on Civil Disorders summarized one view of the situation in two words: "white racism." The commission's report, which will be praised and denounced more than it is read, contains one paragraph particularly pertinent in characterizing the social context in which Black Power rhetoric occurs. In giving reasons for riots in major cities, the writers of the report discuss several before stating:

Finally, many Negroes have come to believe that they are being exploited politically and economically by the white "power structure." Negroes, like people in poverty everywhere, in fact lack the channels of communication, influence and appeal that traditionally have been available to ethnic minorities within the city and which enabled them —unburdened by color—to scale the walls of the white ghettos in an earlier era. The frustrations of powerlessness have led some to the conviction that there is no effective alternative to violence as a means of expression and redress, as a way of "moving the system." More generally, the result is alienation and hostility toward the institutions of law and government and the white society which controls them. This is reflected in the reach toward racial consciousness and solidarity reflected in the slogan "Black Power."[1]

Although the commission's report has tagged well the principal motivation of Black Power as the "frustrations of powerlessness," the commission seems to take unwarranted comfort in finding parallels in Negro history. It argues that themes similar to Black Power have waxed and waned for more than a hundred years:

The Black Power advocates of today consciously feel that they are the most militant group in the Negro protest movement. Yet they have retreated from a direct confrontation with American society on the issue of integration and, by preaching separatism, unconsciously function as an accommodation to white racism. Much of their economic program, as well as their interest in Negro history, self-help, racial solidarity and separation, is reminiscent of Booker T. Washington. The rhetoric is different, but the programs are remarkably similar.[2]

---

[1] *The Report of the National Advisory Commission on Civil Disorders,* New York, Bantam Books, Inc., 1968, p. 205.

[2] *Ibid.,* p. 235. The whole of Chapter Five, "Rejection and Protest: An Historical Sketch," ought to be read by anyone interested in Black Power.

This passage raises more issues than we can consider here, but several remarks may be relevant to our task of introducing what will follow in this book.

First, having to take any position in a complex situation is apt to place anyone in dilemmas. If a black militant sizes up the situation as one in which tokens are offered which demean him and which seem to indicate that the society which practices tokenism is hypocritical at the very best, what is he to do? If he takes what is offered as first steps, trying to make clear that the offer is not enough and grows out of corruption, he becomes a kind of ungrateful recipient and dubious partner of the un- just. On the other hand, if he pulls apart from the established patterns, he becomes a living argument which justifies violence to the most blatant sort of white racists; the least he earns is a tut-tutting as a trouble maker. The reduction of the dilemmas in which we live is what spawns a vigorous rhetoric. Many advo- cates of Black Power argue that only when black people unite as a separate community can they make their power felt, power that will help build a decent life for themselves and power that may help transform American institutions for the better.

Second, the report takes too lightly the probable potency of Black Power. Among those who cry and those who decry the slogan, many see a more revolutionary impulse in it than does the commission. Although the commission freely admits in the report that the American society practices white racism, it seems fundamentally opposed to a radical criticism of the status quo. The separatist dogma that seems inevitably to interweave what- ever the Black Power advocate discusses is bitterly ironic. In the lexicon of black denunciation, the report associates this dogma with Booker T. Washington and calls Black Power advocates Uncle Toms, of a very peculiar, nearly comically absurd sort.

Third, the passage just quoted offers an example of the per- vasiveness of rhetoric. When the report compares the doctrines of Black Power and Booker T. Washington and states that "the rhetoric is different," it implies that this difference makes little difference. The report stresses the purported similarities in pro- gram. But rhetoric makes a grave difference. If legislatures could somehow enact programs and activate automatic machinery which would make everything move mechanically with no human involvement, one could argue that rhetoric is a superfluous part of experience. But the enacting of programs in a vital democratic system entails persuading others. How others are persuaded will have a good deal to do with whether a program is enacted, with the meaning assigned to the machinery for carrying it out, and hence with the ultimate success or failure of the program.

Perhaps no program envisioned at this moment by any Black Power advocate will become a potent force in the conduct of any important group of Americans. Even so, the climate of opinion in this country has been influenced significantly by the rhetoric of Black Power, and the influence is likely to continue. If so, citizens of this nation are wise to consider carefully the patterns of argument and interpersonal relationships that form Black Power's rhetoric. Few case studies of the way words work in persuasive situations should be more interesting than those growing out of this subject.

Our purpose in this volume is to present, from a rhetorical perspective, some of the words and deeds of Black Power. An entirely different set of materials could have been chosen to introduce the rhetoric of Black Power. One could compile a long shelf of books and articles on the subject. We can make no good arguments for our selections over others that are possible, but we claim that our selections have the scope, variety, and brevity to constitute a meaningful introduction.

James P. Comer's "The Social Power of the Negro" presents an insight into the social circumstances from which the slogan springs and on which it focuses. Although no single essay supplies a sufficient background against which to see the movement, Comer's ought to be a good start for some and an interesting variation for others.

The chapter on Black Power from Martin Luther King, Jr.'s last book, *Where Do We Go From Here: Chaos or Community?*, provides further background on the origins of the controversy. King's observations are unique because he fulfills the roles of both reporter and participant. His opposition to the new militancy and his understanding sympathy for the militants are both clear. Although he might not have used the term in quite the sense we do, King was a perceptive rhetorical critic: He looked analytically at the persuasive potential of the slogan and at the ways it might shape those who used it and those who heard it.

The reactions to the cry for Black Power, after it gained widespread public attention during the June, 1966, Meredith March in Mississippi, were immediate. That July at the CORE convention on the East Coast and the NAACP convention on the West, Black Power became the issue which dominated the press reports of the proceedings. In volatile circumstances, Hubert H. Humphrey, an outstanding political speaker, spoke to the NAACP convention. Humphrey was not the first person to suggest that Black Power was racism in reverse, but his endorsement of the idea put the power of the Johnson administration behind an identification of Black Power with the disease which great leaders and powerful institutions, at least publicly, were pledged to cure. The Humphrey speech is representative of a number which draw rather sharp battle lines early in the public campaigns for and against Black Power.

In a book with this title, Stokely Carmichael's voice has to be heard. No person is more closely linked with the slogan than he. We have selected two speeches by Carmichael. One, before a black audience in Detroit, is a rather bristling speech of the kind that may have fixed for many the meaning of Black Power. The other, to a predominantly white audience, invites a very different interpretation. These two speeches, with strikingly similar thought patterns, represent Carmichael's attempt during the latter half of 1966 and the first part of 1967 to adapt a Black Power rhetoric to black and white audiences. In recent months he seems to have become disenchanted with trying to make Black Power coherent to white audiences.

Many would argue that Martin Luther King, Jr., was the outstanding Negro spokesman of the twentieth century. No other person so dominated the attention of such a large portion of the population. The impact of Black Power is revealed dramatically in the influence it apparently had on Dr. King's thinking and speaking. At least this is the way we read the last address he made to an annual convention of the Southern Christian Leadership Conference.

Charles V. Hamilton, the college professor who collaborated with Carmichael in writing *Black Power: The Politics of Liberation in America,* represents a potentiality in Black Power which Carmichael might have actualized but now probably will not. Whether Black Power can become a diverse force, working moderately but effectively to build social and economic institutions with which black men and women can identify, while working also to bring deep changes in the structure of American life, it is too early to judge. But the picture Hamilton draws is a compelling one although it is much less newsworthy than the hysterical shouts that bracket riots. The exposure of Hamilton's recent essay on Black Power in *The New York Times Magazine* will not produce the immediate effect on the general public that film clips on the ten o'clock television news do.

Interspersed among these materials are four critical essays we have written during the past two years. They constitute, of course, not *the* rhetoric of Black Power, but *an* interpretation of that rhetoric. From the chaos of labeling and defining, challenging and accusing, dividing and unifying, a variety of interpretations are possible. Ours is one; we invite you to make others. Our attempts to understand the rhetoric of Black Power may be instructive not only of the subject under scrutiny but of such attempts at critical analysis. Although some of our judgments ought to be modified in light of ongoing Black Power rhetoric, to revise the essays now would be misleading. If we invite others to engage in contemporary criticism of an unfolding rhetoric, we must take our risks in fulfilling the same task.

The critic attempts to understand the forces that form the body of discourse in which he is interested and those forces which in turn are formed out of it. He tries to communicate his understanding to others, encouraging them to see as he sees. The criticism of current rhetoric can become a rhetorical controversy of its own. Anyone who undertakes criticism has to assume responsibility for it. Under some circumstances criticism might be disinterested, objective, and noncontroversial; at this time the criticism of the rhetoric of Black Power can scarcely be so.

## CHAPTER TWO

## *The Social Power of the Negro*

*James P. Comer*

James P. Comer is a fellow in psychiatry at the Yale University School of Medicine. The son of poor laboring parents from the "black belt" of the South, he grew up in East Chicago and graduated from the Howard University School of Medicine. He studied public health at Harvard and Michigan before going to Yale. "My interest in race relations," he wrote for the issue of the *Scientific American* in which his article was first published (April, 1967), "developed at an early age, in part from both troublesome and satisfying experiences...in a low-income family in a racially integrated community."

Mr. Comer's essay appeared less than a year after Black Power became a national issue. It represents a scholarly analysis clearly intended, judging by the style and source of publication, for a highly educated audience.

Although we include it here to serve as a frame of reference for much of the argument that follows in other selections, one ought not overlook the potency of the essay as rhetoric. Although Mr. Comer could expect only a relatively small immediate audience, his potential readers would probably have more than an average impact on the opinions of those with whom they associate. They are, moreover, the sort of persons who would be open to the way in which Comer interprets data.

Elihu Katz and Paul F. Lazarsfeld[1] demonstrated in an often cited study that a two-step flow of communication influences significantly the opinions held in a community. Opinion leaders tend to read and interpret materials, passing information, and especially interpretations, along to their acquaintances. The personal attribute of the relayed opinions is apparently instrumental in the impact they have on the attitudes of these who are thus exposed.

SOURCE: This essay appeared in *Scientific American*, April, 1967, pp. 21–27. Reprinted with permission. Copyright © 1967 by Scientific American, Inc. All rights reserved.

1 *Personal Influence*, New York, The Free Press, 1955.

The concept of black power is an inflammatory one. It was introduced in an atmosphere of militancy . . . and in many quarters it has been equated with violence and riots. As a result the term distresses white friends of the Negro, frightens and angers others and causes many Negroes who are fearful of white disapproval to reject the concept without considering its rationale and its merits. The fact is that a form of black power may be absolutely essential. The experience of Negro Americans, supported by numerous historical and psychological studies, suggests that the profound needs of the poorest and most alienated Negroes cannot be met—and that there can therefore be no end to racial unrest—except through the influence of a unified, organized Negro community with genuine political and economic power.

Why are Negro efforts to achieve greater unity and power considered unnecessary and even dangerous by so many people, Negro as well as white, friends as well as enemies? I believe it is because the functions of group power—and hence the consequences of political and economic impotence—are not understood by most Americans. The "melting pot" myth has obscured the critical role of group power in the adjustment of white immigrant groups in this country. When immigrants were faced with discrimination, exploitation and abuse, they turned in on themselves. Sustained psychologically by the bonds of their cultural heritage, they maintained family, religious and social institutions that had great stabilizing force. The institutions in turn fostered group unity. Family stability and group unity—plus access to political machinery, jobs in industry and opportunities on the frontier—led to group power: immigrants voted, gained political influence, held public office, owned land and operated businesses. Group power and influence expanded individual opportunities and facilitated individual achievement, and within one or two generations most immigrants enjoyed the benefits of first-class American citizenship.

The Negro experience has been very different, as I shall attempt to show in this article. The traumatic effects of separation from Africa, slavery and the denial of political and economic opportunities after the abolition of slavery created divisive psychological and social forces in the Negro community. Coordinated group action, which was certainly appropriate for a despised minority, has been too little evident; Negroes have seldom moved cohesively and effectively against discrimination and exploitation. These abuses led to the creation of an impoverished, undereducated and alienated group—a sizable minority among Negroes, disproportionately large compared with other ethnic groups. This troubled minority has a self-defeating "style" of life that leads to repeated failure, and its plight and its reaction to that plight are at the core of the continuing racial conflict in the U.S. Only a meaningful and powerful Negro community can help members of this group realize their potential, and thus alleviate racial unrest. The importance of black power becomes comprehensible in the light of the interrelation of disunity, impotence and alienation.

The roots of Negro division are of African origin. It is important to realize that the slave contingents brought out of Africa were not from a single ethnic group. They were from a number of groups and from many different tribes with different languages, customs, traditions and ways of life. Some were farmers, some hunters and gatherers, some traders. There were old animosities, and these were exacerbated by the dynamics of the slave trade itself. (Today these same tribal animosities are evident, as in Nigeria, where centuries-old conflict among the Ibo, Hausa and Yoruba tribes threatens to disrupt the nation. A significant number of slaves came from these very tribes.)

The cohesive potential of the captives was low to begin with, and the breakup of kinship groupings, which in Africa had defined people's roles and relations, decreased it further. Presumably if the Africans had been settled in a free land, they would in time have organized to build a new society meeting their own needs. Instead they were organized to meet the needs of their masters. The slaves were scattered in small groups (the average holding was only between two and five slaves) that were isolated from one another. The small number and mixed origins of each plantation's slaves made the maintenance of any oral tradition, and thus of any tribal or racial identity and pride, impossible. Moreover, any grouping that was potentially cohesive because of family, kinship or tribal connections was deliberately divided or tightly controlled to prevent rebellion. Having absolute power, the master could buy and sell, could decree cohabitation, punishment or death, could provide food, shelter and clothing as he saw fit. The system was engraved in law and maintained by the religious and political authorities and the armed forces; the high visibility of the slaves and the lack of places to hide made escape almost inconceivable.

The powerless position of the slave was traumatic, as Stanley M. Elkins showed in his study of Negro slavery. The male was not the respected provider, the protector and head of his household. The female was not rearing her child to take his place in a rewarding society, nor could she count on protection from her spouse or any responsible male. The reward for hard work was not material goods and the recognition of one's fellow men but only recognition from the master as a faithful but inferior being. The master—"the man"—became the necessary object of the slave's emotional investment, the person whose approval he needed. The slave could love or hate or have ambivalent feelings about the relationship, but it was the most important relationship of his life.

In this situation self-esteem depended on closeness or similarity to the master, not on personal or group power and achievement, and it was gained in ways that tended to divide the Negro population. House slaves looked down on field hands, "mixed-bloods" on "pure blacks," slaves with rich and important masters on slaves whose masters had less prestige. There was cleavage between the "troublemakers" who promoted revolt and sabotage and the "good slaves" who betrayed them, and between slave Negroes and free ones. The development of positive identity as a Negro was scarcely possible.

It is often assumed that with the end of the Civil War the situation of the free Negroes was about the same as that of immigrants landing in America. In reality it was quite different. Negroes emerging from slavery entered a society at a peak of racial antagonism. They had long since been stripped of their African heritage; in their years in America they had been unable to create much of a record of their own; they were deeply marked by the degrading experience of slavery. Most significant, they were denied the weapons they needed to become part of American life: economic and political opportunities. No longer of any value to their former masters, they were now direct competitors of the poor whites. The conditions of life imposed by the "Black codes" of the immediate postwar period were in many ways as harsh as slavery had been. In the first two years after the end of the war many Negroes suffered violence and death at the hands of unrestrained whites; there was starvation and extreme dislocation.

In 1867 the Reconstruction Acts put the South under military occupation and gave freedmen in the 11 Southern states the right to vote. (In the North, on the other hand, Negroes continued to be barred from the polls in all but nine states, either by specific racial qualifications or by prohibitive taxation. Until the Fifteenth Amendment was ratified in 1870, only some 5 percent of the Northern Negroes could vote.) The Reconstruction Acts also provided some military and legal protection, educational opportunities and health care. Reconstruction did not, however, make enough land available to Negroes to create an adequate power base. The plantation system meant that large numbers of Negroes remained under tight control and were vulnerable to economic reprisals. Although Negroes could outvote whites in some states and did in fact control the Louisiana and South Carolina legislatures, the franchise did not lead to real power.

This lack of power was largely due to the Negro's economic vulnerability, but the group divisions that had developed during slavery also played a part. It was the "mixed-bloods" and the house slaves of middle- and upper-class whites who had acquired some education and skills under slavery; now many of these people became Negro leaders. They often had emotional ties to whites and a need to please them, and they advanced the cause of the Negroes as a group most gingerly. Moreover, not understanding the causes of the apathy, lack of achievement and asocial behavior of some of their fellows, many of them found their Negro identity a source of shame rather than psychological support, and they were ready to subordinate the needs of the group to personal gains that would give them as much social and psychological distance from their people as possible. The result was that Negro leaders, with some notable exceptions, often became the tools of white leaders. Throughout the Reconstruction period meaningful Negro power was being destroyed, and long before the last Negro disappeared from Southern legislatures Negroes were powerless.

Under such circumstances Negro economic and educational progress was severely inhibited. Negro-owned businesses were largely dependent on the impoverished Negro community and were operated by people who had little education or experience and who found it difficult to secure financing; they could not compete with white businesses. Negroes were largely untrained for anything but farm labor or domestic work, and a white social structure maintaining itself through physical force and economic exploitation was not likely to provide the necessary educational opportunities. Minimal facilities, personnel and funds were provided for the "Negro schools" that were established, and only the most talented Negroes were able—if they were lucky—to obtain an education comparable to that available to whites.

As John Hope Franklin describes it in *Reconstruction after the Civil War*, the Reconstruction was ineffective for the vast majority of Negroes, and it lasted only a short time: Federal troops had left most Southern states by 1870. While Negroes were still struggling for a first foothold, national political developments made it advisable to placate Southern leaders, and the Federal troops were recalled from the last three Southern states in 1877. There was a brief period of restraint, but it soon gave way to violence and terror on a large scale. Threats and violence drove Negroes away from the polls. Racist sheriffs, legislators and judges came into office. Segregation laws were passed, buttressed by court decisions and law enforcement practices and erected into an institution that rivaled slavery in its effectiveness in excluding Negroes from public affairs—business, the labor movement, government and public education.

At the time—and in later years—white people often pointed to the most depressed and unstable Negro and in effect made his improvement in education and behavior a condition for the granting of equal opportunities to all Negroes. What kind of people made up this most disadvantaged segment of the Negro community? I believe it can be shown that these were the Negroes who had lived under the most traumatic and disorganized conditions as slaves. Family life had been prohibited, discouraged or allowed to exist only under precarious conditions, with no recourse from sale, separation or sexual violation. Some of these people had been treated as breeding stock or work animals; many had experienced brutal and sadistic physical and sexual assaults. In many cases the practice of religion was forbidden, so that even self-respect as "a child of God" was denied them.

Except for running away (and more tried to escape than has generally been realized) there was nothing these slaves could do but adopt various defense mechanisms. They responded in various ways, as is poignantly recorded in a collection of first-hand accounts obtained by Benjamin A. Botkin. Many did as little work as they could without being punished, thus developing work habits that were not conducive to success after slavery. Many sabotaged the master's tools and other property, thus evolving a disrespect for property in general. Some resorted to a massive denial of the reality of their lives and took refuge in apathy, thus creating the slow-moving, slow-thinking stereotype of the Southern Negro. Others resorted instead to boisterous "acting out" behavior and limited their interests to the fulfillment of such basic needs as food and sex.

After slavery these patterns of behavior persisted. The members of this severely traumatized group did not value family life. Moreover, for economic reasons and by force of custom the family often lacked a male head, or at least a legal husband and father. Among these people irresponsibility, poor work habits, disregard for conventional standards and anger toward whites expressed in violence toward one another combined to form a way of life—a style—that caused them to be rejected and despised by whites and other Negroes alike. They were bound to fail in the larger world.

When they did fail, they turned in on their own subculture, which accordingly became self-reinforcing. Children born into it learned its way of life. Isolated and also insulated from outside influences, they had little opportunity to change. The values, behavior patterns and sense of alienation transmitted within this segment of the population from generation to generation account for the bulk of the illegitimacy, crime and other types of asocial behavior that are present in disproportionate amounts in the Negro community today. This troubled subgroup has always been a minority, but its behavior constitutes many white people's concept of "typical" Negro behavior and even tarnishes the image many other Negroes have of themselves. Over the years defensive Negro leaders have regularly blamed the depressed subgroup for creating a bad image; the members of the subgroup have blamed the leaders for "selling out." There has been just enough truth in both accusations to keep them alive, accentuating division and perpetuating conflicts, and impeding the development of group consciousness, cooperation, power and mutual gains.

It is surprising, considering the harsh conditions of slavery, that there were any Negroes who made a reasonable adjustment to freedom. Many had come from Africa with a set of values that included hard work and stability of family and tribal life. (I suspect, but I have not been able to demonstrate, that in Africa many of these had been farmers rather than hunters and gatherers.) As slaves many of them found the support and rewards required to maintain such values through their intense involvement in religion. From this group, after slavery, came the God-fearing, hardworking, law-abiding domestics and laborers who prepared their children for responsible living, in many cases making extreme personal sacrifices to send them to trade school or college. (The significance of this church-oriented background in motivating educational effort and success even today is indicated by some preliminary findings of a compensatory education program for which I am a consultant. Of 125 Negro students picked for the program from 10 southeastern states solely on the basis of academic promise, 95 percent have parents who are regular churchgoers, deeply involved as organizers and leaders in church affairs.)

For a less religious group of Negroes the discovery of meaning, fulfillment and a sense of worth lay in a different direction. Their creative talents brought recognition in the arts, created the blues and jazz and opened the entertainment industry to Negroes. Athletic excellence provided another kind of achievement. Slowly, from among the religious, the creative and the athletic, a new, educated and talented middle class began to emerge that had less need of white approval than the Negroes who had managed to get ahead in earlier days. Large numbers of Negroes should have risen into the middle class by way of these relatively stable groups, but because of the lack of Negro political and economic power and the barriers of racial prejudice many could not. Those whose aspirations were frustrated often reacted destructively by turning to the depressed Negro subgroup and its way of life; the subculture of failure shaped by slavery gained new recruits and was perpetuated by a white society's obstacles to acceptance and achievement.

In the past 10 years or so the "Negro revolt"—the intensified legal actions, nonviolent demonstrations, court decisions and legislation—and changing economic conditions have brought rapid and significant gains for middle-class Negroes. The mass of low-income Negroes have made little progress, however; many have been aroused by civil rights talk but few have benefited. Of all Negro families, 40 percent are classified as "poor" according to Social Security Administration criteria. (The figure for white families is 11 percent.) Low-income Negroes have menial jobs or are unemployed; they live in segregated neighborhoods and are exploited by landlords and storekeepers; they are often the victims of crime and of the violent, displaced frustration of their friends and neighbors. The urban riots of the past few years have been the reaction of a small segment of this population to the frustrations of its daily existence.

Why is it that so many Negroes have been unable to take advantage of the Negro revolt as the immigrants did of opportunities offered them? The major reason is that the requirements for economic success have been raised. The virtually free land on the frontier is gone. The unskilled and semiskilled jobs that were available to white immigrants are scarce today, and many unions controlled by lower-middle-class whites bar Negroes to keep the jobs for their present members. The law does not help here because Negroes are underrepresented in municipal and state legislative bodies as well as in Congress. Negroes hold few policy-making positions in industry and Negro small businesses are a negligible source of employment.

Employment opportunities exist, of course—for highly skilled workers and technicians. These jobs require education and training that many Negroes, along with many white workers, lack. The training takes time and requires motivation, and it must be based on satisfactory education through high school. Most poor Negroes lack that education, and many young Negroes are not getting it today. There are Negro children who are performing adequately in elementary school but who will fail by the time they reach high school, either because their schools are inadequate or because their homes and subculture will simply not sustain their efforts in later years.

It is not enough to provide a "head start"; studies have shown that gains made as the result of the new preschool enrichment programs are lost, in most cases, by the third grade. Retraining programs for workers and programs for high school dropouts are palliative measures that have limited value. Some of the jobs for which people are being trained will not exist in a few years. Many students drop out of the dropout programs. Other students have such self-defeating values and behavior that they will not be employable even if they complete the programs.

A number of investigators (Daniel P. Moynihan is one) have pointed to the structure of the poorer Negro family as the key to Negro problems. They point to an important area but miss the crux of the problem. Certainly the lack of a stable family deprives many Negro children of psychological security and of the values and behavior patterns they need in order to achieve success. Certainly many low-income Negro families lack a father. Even if it were possible to legislate the father back into the home, however, the grim picture is unchanged if his own values and conduct are not compatible with achievement. A father frustrated by society often reacts by mistreating his children. Even adequate parents despair and are helpless in a subculture that leads their children astray. The point of intervention must be the subculture that impinges on the family and influences its values and style of behavior and even its structure.

How, then, does one break the circle? Many white children who found their immigrant family and subculture out of step with the dominant American culture and with their own desires were able to break away and establish a sense of belonging to a group outside their own—if the pull was strong enough. Some children in the depressed Negro group do this too. A specific pull is often needed: some individual or institution that sets a goal or acts as a model. The trouble is that racial prejudice and alienation from the white and Negro middle class often mean that there is little pull from the dominant culture on lower-class Negro children. In my work in schools in disadvantaged areas as a consultant from the Child Study Center of Yale University I have found that many Negro children perceive the outside culture as a separate white man's world. Once they are 12 or 14 years old—the age at which a firm sense of racial identity is established—many Negroes have a need to shut out the white man's world and its values and institutions and also to reject "white Negroes," or the Negro middle class. Since these children see their problems as being racial ones, they are more likely to learn how to cope with these problems from a middle-class Negro who extends himself than from a white person, no matter how honest and free of hostility and guilt the white person may be.

Unfortunately the Negro community is not now set up to offer its disadvantaged members a set of standards and a psychological refuge in the way the white immigrant subcultures did. There is no Negro institution beyond the family that is enough in harmony with the total American culture to transmit its behavioral principles and is meaningful enough to Negroes to effect adherence to those principles and sufficiently accepted by divergent elements of the Negro community to act as a cohesive force. The church comes closest to performing this function, but Negroes belong to an exceptional number of different denominations, and in many cases the denominations are divided and antagonistic. The same degree of division is found in the major fraternal and civic organizations and even in civil rights groups.

There is a special reason for some of the sharp divisions in Negro organizations. With Negroes largely barred from business, politics and certain labor unions, the quest for power and leadership in Negro organizations has been and continues to be particularly intense, and there is a great deal of conflict. Only a few Negroes have a broad enough view of the total society to be able to identify the real sources of their difficulties. And the wide divergence of their interests often makes it difficult for them to agree on a course of action. All these factors make Negro groups vulnerable to divide-and-conquer tactics, either inadvertent or deliberate.

Viewing such disarray, altruistic white people and public and private agencies have moved into the apparent vacuum—often failing to recognize that, in spite of conflict, existing Negro institutions were meeting important psychological needs and were in close contact with their people. Using these meaningful institutions as vehicles for delivering new social services would have strengthened the only forces capable of supporting and organizing the Negro community. Instead the new agencies, public and private, have ignored the existing institutions and have tried to do the job themselves. The agencies often have storefront locations and hire some "indigenous" workers, but the class and racial gap is difficult to cross. The thong-sandaled, long-haired white girl doing employment counseling may be friendly and sympathetic to Negroes, but she cannot possibly tell a Negro youngster (indeed, she does not know that she should tell him): "You've got to look better than the white applicant to get the job." Moreover, a disadvantaged Negro—or any Negro—repeatedly helped by powerful white people while his own group appears powerless or unconcerned is unlikely to develop satisfactory feelings about his group or himself. The effects of an undesirable racial self-concept among many Negroes have been documented repeatedly, yet many current programs tend to perpetuate this basic problem rather than to relieve it.

A solution is suggested by the fact that many successful

Negroes no longer feel the need to maintain psychological and social distance from their own people. Many of them want to help. Their presence and tangible involvement in the Negro community would tend to balance the pull—the comforts and the immediate pleasures—of the subculture. Because the functions of Negro organizations have been largely preempted by white agencies, however, no Negro institution is available through which such people can work to overcome a century of intra-Negro class alienation.

Recently a few Negroes have begun to consider a plan that could meet some of the practical needs, as well as the spiritual and psychological needs, of the Negro community. In Cleveland, New York, Los Angeles and some smaller cities new leaders are emerging who propose to increase Negro cohesiveness and self-respect through self-help enterprises: cooperatives that would reconstruct slums or operate apartment buildings and businesses providing goods and services at fair prices. Ideally these enterprises would be owned by people who mean something to the Negro community—Negro athletes, entertainers, artists, professionals and government workers—and by Negro churches, fraternal groups and civil rights organizations. The owners would share control of the enterprises with the people of the community.

Such undertakings would be far more than investment opportunities for well-to-do Negroes. With the proper structure they would become permanent and tangible institutions on which the Negro community could focus without requiring a "white enemy" and intolerable conditions to unify it. Through this mechanism Negroes who had achieved success could come in contact with the larger Negro group. Instead of the policy king, pimp and prostitute being the models of success in the subculture, the Negro athlete, businessman, professional and entertainer might become the models once they could be respected because they were obviously working for the Negro community. These leaders would then be in a position to encourage and promote high-level performance in school and on the job. At the same time broad measures to "institutionalize" the total Negro experience would increase racial pride, a powerful motivating force. The entire program would provide the foundation for unified political action to give the Negro community representatives who speak in its best interests.

That, after all, has been the pattern in white America. There was, and still is, Irish power, German, Polish, Italian and Jewish power—and indeed white Anglo-Saxon Protestant power—but color obviously makes these groups less clearly identifiable than Negroes. Churches and synagogues, cultural and fraternal societies, unions, business associations and networks of allied families and "clans" have served as centers of power that maintain group consciousness, provide jobs and develop new opportunities and join to form pressure and voting blocs. The "nationality divisions" of the major parties and the balanced ticket are two reminders that immigrant loyalties are still not completely melted.

The idea of creating Negro enterprises and institutions is not intended as a rejection of genuinely concerned white people or as an indictment of all existing organizations. White people of good will with interest, skills and funds are needed and—contrary to the provocative assertions of a few Negroes—are still welcome in the Negro community. The kind of black power that is proposed would not promote riots; rather, by providing constructive channels for the energies released by the civil rights movement, it should diminish the violent outbursts directed against the two symbols of white power and oppression: the police and the white merchants.

To call for Negro institutions, moreover, is not to argue for segregation or discrimination. Whether we like it or not, a number of large cities are going to become predominantly Negro in a short time. The aim is to make these cities places where people can live decently and reach their highest potential with or without integration. An integrated society is the ultimate goal, but it may be a second stage in some areas. Where immediate integration is possible it should be effected, but integration takes place most easily among educated and secure people. And in the case of immediate integration an organized and supportive Negro community would help its members to maintain a sense of adequacy in a situation in which repeated reminders of the white head start often make Negroes feel all the more inferior.

The power structure of white society—industry, banks, the press, government—can continue, either inadvertently or deliberately, to maintain the divisions in the Negro community and keep it powerless. Social and economic statistics and psychological studies indicate that this would be a mistake. For many reasons the ranks of the alienated are growing. No existing program seems able to meet the needs of the most troubled and troublesome group. It is generally agreed that massive, immediate action is required. The form of that action should be attuned, however, to the historically determined need for Negro political and economic power that will facilitate Negro progress and give Negroes a reasonable degree of control over their own destiny.

# CHAPTER THREE

## *Martin Luther King, Jr., Writes About the Birth of the Black Power Slogan*

On April 4, 1968, in Memphis, Tennessee, where he had gone to support a strike by municipal garbage collection workers, Martin Luther King, Jr., was struck down by an assassin's bullet. Thus a great apostle of nonviolent resistance to evil, a winner of the Nobel Peace Prize, died violently. Horror was registered by a multitude, from the humble to the well-established mighty. Declarations of renewed good intentions and calls for reinvigorated efforts echoed throughout the nation. An editorialist for *The New York Times* wrote:

> Seldom in its history has this country been ... so shocked, as it has been by the death of Martin Luther King. Seldom in its history has this country had a leader of such transcendent spirit combined with iron will, of such integrity of purpose combined with magnetic appeal, of such devotion to a great cause combined with the courage to pursue it.
>
> Martin Luther King, the man of peace, evoked the very best in Americans of every race and creed; and the tremendous outpouring of silent and spoken grief that centered yesterday in Atlanta gave expression to the overwhelming sentiment of a stunned and united nation. United? It must be united.
>
> This is the legacy of Martin Luther King, as it was his vision. The people of this country cannot fail him now. The concept of racial inferiority and racial discrimination is intolerable if the United States is to survive. It is the fundamental question, and Dr. King, apostle of brotherhood, understood it as such. With all its power and all its majesty, this nation must move to make his vision a reality.[1]

SOURCE: "Black Power" is the second chapter of Dr. King's book *Where Do We Go from Here: Chaos or Community?* (New York, Harper & Row, Publishers, 1967). Copyright © 1967, by Martin Luther King, Jr. Reprinted by permission of the publisher.

[1] *The New York Times*, Apr. 10, 1968, p. 46. Copyright © 1968, by The New York Times Company. Quoted by permission.

How those with power will respond to such calls as this one is not yet clear. Nor is it clear that the public generally has a disposition to make the weight of opinion fall decisively on the levers of democratic action. But it is clear that the nation has faced few tests of the vitality of its ideals more crucial than those that the life and death of this man pose.


"James Meredith has been shot!"

It was about three o'clock in the afternoon on a Monday in June, 1966, and I was presiding over the regular staff meeting of the Southern Christian Leadership Conference in our Atlanta headquarters. When we heard that Meredith had been shot in the back only a day after he had begun his Freedom March through Mississippi, there was a momentary hush of anger and dismay throughout the room. Our horror was compounded by the fact that the early reports announced that Meredith was dead. Soon the silence was broken, and from every corner of the room came expressions of outrage. The business of the meeting was forgotten in the shock of this latest evidence that a Negro's life is still worthless in many parts of his own country.

When order was finally restored, our executive staff immediately agreed that the march must continue. After all, we reasoned, Meredith had begun his lonely journey as a pilgrimage against fear. Wouldn't failure to continue only intensify the fears of the oppressed and deprived Negroes of Mississippi? Would this not be a setback for the whole civil rights movement and a blow to nonviolent discipline?

After several calls between Atlanta and Memphis, we learned that the earlier reports of Meredith's death were false and that he would recover. This news brought relief, but it did not alter our feeling that the civil rights movement had a moral obligation to continue along the path that Meredith had begun.

The next morning I was off to Memphis along with several members of my staff. Floyd McKissick, National Director of CORE, flew in from New York and joined us on the flight from Atlanta to Memphis. After landing we went directly to the Municipal Hospital to visit Meredith. We were happy to find him resting well. After expressing our sympathy and gratitude for his courageous witness, Floyd and I shared our conviction with him that the march should continue in order to demonstrate to the nation and the world that Negroes would never again be intimidated by the terror of extremist white violence. Realizing that Meredith was often a loner and that he probably wanted to continue the march without a large group, we felt that it would take a great deal of persuasion to convince him that the issue involved the whole civil rights movement. Fortunately, he soon saw this and agreed that we should continue without him. We spent some time discussing the character and logistics of the march, and agreed that we would consult with him daily on every decision.

As we prepared to leave, the nurse came to the door and said, "Mr. Meredith, there is a Mr. Carmichael in the lobby who would like to see you and Dr. King. Should I give him permission to come in?" Meredith consented. Stokely Carmichael entered with his associate, Cleveland Sellers, and immediately reached out for Meredith's hand. He expressed his concern and admiration and brought messages of sympathy from his colleagues in the Student Nonviolent Coordinating Committee. After a brief conversation we all agreed that James should get some rest and that we should not burden him with any additional talk. We left the room assuring him that we would conduct the march in his spirit and would seek as never before to expose the ugly racism that pervaded Mississippi and to arouse a new sense of dignity and manhood in every Negro who inhabited that bastion of man's inhumanity to man.

In a brief conference Floyd, Stokely and I agreed that the march would be jointly sponsored by CORE, SNCC and SCLC, with the understanding that all other civil rights organizations would be invited to join. It was also agreed that we would issue a national call for support and participation.

One hour later, after making staff assignments and setting up headquarters at the Rev. James Lawson's church in Memphis, a group of us packed into four automobiles and made our way to that desolate spot on Highway 51 where James

Meredith had been shot the day before. So began the second stage of the Meredith Mississippi Freedom March.

As we walked down the meandering highway in the sweltering heat, there was much talk and many questions were raised.

"I'm not for that nonviolence stuff any more," shouted one of the younger activists.

"If one of these damn white Mississippi crackers touches me, I'm gonna knock the hell out of him," shouted another.

Later on a discussion of the composition of the march came up.

"This should be an all-black march," said one marcher. "We don't need any more white phonies and liberals invading our movement. This is our march."

Once during the afternoon we stopped to sing "We Shall Overcome." The voices rang out with all the traditional fervor, the glad thunder and gentle strength that had always characterized the singing of this noble song. But when we came to the stanza which speaks of "black and white together," the voices of a few of the marchers were muted. I asked them later why they refused to sing that verse. The retort was:

"This is a new day, we don't sing those words any more. In fact, the whole song should be discarded. Not 'We Shall Overcome,' but 'We Shall Overrun.'"

As I listened to all these comments, the words fell on my ears like strange music from a foreign land. My hearing was not attuned to the sound of such bitterness. I guess I should not have been surprised. I should have known that in an atmosphere where false promises are daily realities, where deferred dreams are nightly facts, where acts of unpunished violence toward Negroes are a way of life, nonviolence would eventually be seriously questioned. I should have been reminded that disappointment produces despair and despair produces bitterness, and that the one thing certain about bitterness is its blindness. Bitterness has not the capacity to make the distinction between some and *all*. When some members of the dominant group, particularly those in power, are racist in attitude and practice, bitterness accuses the whole group.

At the end of the march that first day we all went back to

Memphis and spent the night in a Negro motel, since we had not yet secured the tents that would serve as shelter each of the following nights on our journey. The discussion continued at the motel. I decided that I would plead patiently with my brothers to remain true to the time-honored principles of our movement. I began with a plea for nonviolence. This immediately aroused some of our friends from the Deacons for Defense, who contended that self-defense was essential and that therefore nonviolence should not be a prerequisite for participation in the march. They were joined in this view by some of the activists from CORE and SNCC.

I tried to make it clear that besides opposing violence on principle, I could imagine nothing more impractical and disastrous than for any of us, through misguided judgment, to precipitate a violent confrontation in Mississippi. We had neither the resources nor the techniques to win. Furthermore, I asserted, many Mississippi whites, from the government on down, would enjoy nothing more than for us to turn to violence in order to use this as an excuse to wipe out scores of Negroes in and out of the march. Finally, I contended that the debate over the question of self-defense was unnecessary since few people suggested that Negroes should not defend themselves as individuals when attacked. The question was not whether one should use his gun when his home was attacked, but whether it was tactically wise to use a gun while participating in an organized demonstration. If they lowered the banner of nonviolence, I said, Mississippi injustice would not be exposed and the moral issues would be obscured.

Next the question of the participation of whites was raised. Stokely Carmichael contended that the inclusion of whites in the march should be de-emphasized and that the dominant appeal should be made for black participation. Others in the room agreed. As I listened to Stokely, I thought about the years that we had worked together in communities all across the South, and how joyously we had then welcomed and accepted our white allies in the movement. What accounted for this reversal in Stokely's philosophy?

I surmised that much of the change had its psychological

roots in the experience of SNCC in Mississippi during the summer of 1964, when a large number of Northern white students had come down to help in that racially torn state. What the SNCC workers saw was the most articulate, powerful and self-assured young white people coming to work with the poorest of the Negro people—and simply overwhelming them. That summer Stokely and others in SNCC had probably unconsciously concluded that this was no good for Negroes, for it simply increased their sense of their own inadequacies. Of course, the answer to this dilemma was not to give up, not to conclude that blacks must work with blacks in order for Negroes to gain a sense of their own meaning. The answer was only to be found in persistent trying, perpetual experimentation, persevering togetherness.

Like life, racial understanding is not something that we find but something that we must create. What we find when we enter these mortal plains is existence; but existence is the raw material out of which all life must be created. A productive and happy life is not something that you find; it is something that you make. And so the ability of Negroes and whites to work together, to understand each other, will not be found ready made; it must be created by the fact of contact.

Along these lines, I implored everyone in the room to see the morality of making the march completely interracial. Consciences must be enlisted in our movement, I said, not merely racial groups. I reminded them of the dedicated whites who had suffered, bled and died in the cause of racial justice, and suggested that to reject white participation now would be a shameful repudiation of all for which they had sacrificed.

Finally, I said that the formidable foe we now faced demanded more unity than ever before and that I would stretch every point to maintain this unity, but that I could not in good conscience agree to continue my personal involvement and that of SCLC in the march if it were not publicly affirmed that it was based on nonviolence and the participation of both black and white. After a few more minutes of discussion Floyd and Stokely agreed that we could unite around these principles as far as the march was concerned. The next morning we had a joint press conference affirming that the march was non-violent and that whites were welcomed.

As the days progressed, debates and discussions continued, but they were usually pushed to the background by the onrush of enthusiasm engendered by the large crowds that turned out to greet us in every town. We had been marching for about ten days when we passed through Grenada on the way to Greenwood. Stokely did not conceal his growing eagerness to reach Greenwood. This was SNCC territory, in the sense that the organization had worked courageously there during that turbulent summer of 1964.

As we approached the city, large crowds of old friends and new turned out to welcome us. At a huge mass meeting that night, which was held in a city park, Stokely mounted the platform and after arousing the audience with a powerful attack on Mississippi justice, he proclaimed: "What we need is Black Power." Willie Ricks, the fiery orator of SNCC, leaped to the platform and shouted, "What do you want?" The crowd roared, "Black Power." Again and again Ricks cried, "What do you want?" and the response "Black Power" grew louder and louder, until it had reached fever pitch.

So Greenwood turned out to be the arena for the birth of the Black Power slogan in the civil rights movement. The phrase had been used long before by Richard Wright and others, but never until that night had it been used as a slogan in the civil rights movement. For people who had been crushed so long by white power and who had been taught that black was degrading, it had a ready appeal.

Immediately, however, I had reservations about its use. I had the deep feeling that it was an unfortunate choice of words for a slogan. Moreover, I saw it bringing about division within the ranks of the marchers. For a day or two there was fierce competition between those who were wedded to the Black Power slogan and those wedded to Freedom Now. Speakers on each side sought desperately to get the crowds to chant their slogan the loudest.

Sensing this widening split in our ranks, I asked Stokely and Floyd to join me in a frank discussion of the problem.

We met the next morning, along with members of each of our staffs, in a small Catholic parish house in Yazoo City. For five long hours I pleaded with the group to abandon the Black Power slogan. It was my contention that a leader has to be concerned about the problem of semantics. Each word, I said, has a denotative meaning—its explicit and recognized sense—and a connotative meaning—its suggestive sense. While the concept of legitimate Black Power might be denotatively sound, the slogan Black Power carried the wrong connotations. I mentioned the implications of violence that the press had already attached to the phrase. And I went on to say that some of the rash statements on the part of a few marchers only reinforced this impression.

Stokely replied by saying that the question of violence versus nonviolence was irrelevant. The real question was the need for black people to consolidate their political and economic resources to achieve power. "Power," he said, "is the only thing respected in this world, and we must get it at any cost." Then he looked me squarely in the eye and said, "Martin, you know as well as I do that practically every other ethnic group in America has done just this. The Jews, the Irish and the Italians did it, why can't we?"

"That is just the point," I answered. "No one has ever heard the Jews publicly chant a slogan of Jewish power, but they have power. Through group unity, determination and creative endeavor, they have gained it. The same thing is true of the Irish and Italians. Neither group has used a slogan of Irish or Italian power, but they have worked hard to achieve it. This is exactly what we must do," I said. "We must use every constructive means to amass economic and political power. This is the kind of legitimate power we need. We must work to build racial pride and refute the notion that black is evil and ugly. But this must come through a program, not merely through a slogan."

Stokely and Floyd insisted that the slogan itself was important. "How can you arouse people to unite around a program without a slogan as a rallying cry? Didn't the labor movement have slogans? Haven't we had slogans all along in the freedom movement? What we need is a new slogan with 'black' in it."

I conceded the fact that we must have slogans. But why have one that would confuse our allies, isolate the Negro community and give many prejudiced whites, who might otherwise be ashamed of their anti-Negro feeling, a ready excuse for self-justification?

"Why not use the slogan Black Consciousness or Black Equality?" I suggested. "These phrases would be less vulnerable and would more accurately describe what we are about. The words 'black' and 'power' together give the impression that we are talking about black domination rather than black equality."

Stokely responded that neither would have the ready appeal and persuasive force of Black Power. Throughout the lengthy discussion, Stokely and Floyd remained adamant, and Stokely concluded by saying, with candor, "Martin, I deliberately decided to raise this issue on the march in order to give it a national forum, and force you to take a stand for Black Power."

I laughed. "I have been used before," I said to Stokely. "One more time won't hurt."

The meeting ended with the SCLC staff members still agreeing with me that the slogan was unfortunate and would only divert attention from the evils of Mississippi, while most CORE and SNCC staff members joined Stokely and Floyd in insisting that it should be projected nationally. In a final attempt to maintain unity I suggested that we compromise by not chanting either Black Power or Freedom Now for the rest of the march. In this way neither the people nor the press would be confused by the apparent conflict, and staff members would not appear to be at loggerheads. They all agreed with this compromise.

But while the chant died out, the press kept the debate going. News stories now centered, not on the injustices of Mississippi, but on the apparent ideological division in the civil rights movement. Every revolutionary movement has its peaks of united activity and its valleys of debate and internal confusion. This debate might well have been little more than a healthy internal difference of opinion, but the press loves the sensational and it could not allow the issue to remain within the private domain of the movement. In every drama there has to be an antagonist and a protagonist, and if the antagonist is not there the press will find and build one.

## II

So Black Power is now a part of the nomenclature of the national community. To some it is abhorrent, to others dynamic; to some it is repugnant, to others exhilarating; to some it is destructive, to others it is useful. Since Black Power means different things to different people and indeed, being essentially an emotional concept, can mean different things to the same person on differing occasions, it is impossible to attribute its ultimate meaning to any single individual or organization. One must look beyond personal styles, verbal flourishes and the hysteria of the mass media to assess its values, its assets and liabilities honestly.

First, it is necessary to understand that Black Power is a cry of disappointment. The Black Power slogan did not spring full grown from the head of some philosophical Zeus. It was born from the wounds of despair and disappointment. It is a cry of daily hurt and persistent pain. For centuries the Negro has been caught in the tentacles of white power. Many Negroes have given up faith in the white majority because white power with total control has left them empty-handed. So in reality the call for Black Power is a reaction to the failure of white power.

It is no accident that the birth of this slogan in the civil rights movement took place in Mississippi—the state symbolizing the most blatant abuse of white power. In Mississippi the murder of civil rights workers is still a popular pastime. In that state more than forty Negroes and whites have either been lynched or murdered over the last three years, and not a single man has been punished for these crimes. More than fifty Negro churches have been burned or bombed in Mississippi in the last two years, yet the bombers still walk the streets surrounded by the halo of adoration.[2] This is white power in its most brutal, cold-blooded and vicious form.

Many of the young people proclaiming Black Power today were but yesterday the devotees of black-white cooperation and nonviolent direct action. With great sacrifice and dedication and a radiant faith in the future they labored courageously in the rural areas of the South; with idealism they accepted blows without retaliating; with dignity they allowed themselves to be plunged into filthy, stinking jail cells; with a majestic scorn for risk and danger they nonviolently confronted the Jim Clarks and the Bull Connors of the South, and exposed the disease of racism in the body politic. If they are America's angry children today, this anger is not congenital. It is a response to the feeling that a real solution is hopelessly distant because of the inconsistencies, resistance and faintheartedness of those in power. If Stokely Carmichael now says that nonviolence is irrelevant, it is because he, as a dedicated veteran of many battles, has seen with his own eyes the most brutal white violence against Negroes and white civil rights workers, and he has seen it go unpunished.

Their frustration is further fed by the fact that even when blacks and whites die together in the cause of justice, the death of the white person gets more attention and concern than the death of the black person. Stokely and his colleagues from SNCC were with us in Alabama when Jimmy Lee Jackson, a brave young Negro man, was killed and when James Reeb, a committed Unitarian white minister, was fatally clubbed to the ground. They remembered how President Johnson sent flowers to the gallant Mrs. Reeb, and in his eloquent "We Shall Overcome" speech paused to mention that one person, James Reeb, had already died in the struggle. Somehow the President forgot to mention Jimmy, who died first. The parents and sister of Jimmy received no flowers from the President. The students felt this keenly. Not that they felt that the death of James Reeb was less than tragic, but because they felt that the failure to mention Jimmy Jackson only reinforced the

[2] Southern Regional Council, 1966.

impression that to white America the life of a Negro is insignificant and meaningless.

There is also great disappointment with the federal government and its timidity in implementing the civil rights laws on its statute books. The gap between promise and fulfillment is distressingly wide. Millions of Negroes are frustrated and angered because extravagant promises made little more than a year ago are a mockery today. When the 1965 Voting Rights Law was signed, it was proclaimed as the dawn of freedom and the open door to opportunity. What was minimally required under the law was the appointment of hundreds of registrars and thousands of federal marshals to inhibit Southern terror. Instead, fewer than sixty registrars were appointed and not a single federal law officer capable of making arrests was sent into the South. As a consequence the old way of life—economic coercion, terrorism, murder and inhuman contempt— has continued unabated. This gulf between the laws and their enforcement is one of the basic reasons why Black Power advocates express contempt for the legislative process.

The disappointment mounts as they turn their eyes to the North. In the Northern ghettos, unemployment, housing discrimination and slum schools mock the Negro who tries to hope. There have been accomplishments and some material gain, but these beginnings have revealed how far we have yet to go. The economic plight of the masses of Negroes has worsened. The gap between the wages of the Negro worker and those of the white worker has widened. Slums are worse and Negroes attend more thoroughly segregated schools today than in 1954.

The Black Power advocates are disenchanted with the inconsistencies in the militaristic posture of our government. Over the last decade they have seen America applauding nonviolence whenever the Negroes have practiced it. They have watched it being praised in the sit-in movements of 1960, in the Freedom Rides of 1961, in the Albany movement of 1962, in the Birmingham movement of 1963 and in the Selma movement of 1965. But then these same black young men and women have watched as America sends black young men to burn Vietnamese with napalm, to slaughter men, women and children; and they wonder what kind of nation it is that applauds nonviolence whenever Negroes face white people in the streets of the United States but then applauds violence and burning and death when these same Negroes are sent to the field of Vietnam.

All of this represents disappointment lifted to astronomical proportions. It is disappointment with timid white moderates who feel that they can set the timetable for the Negro's freedom. It is disappointment with a federal administration that seems to be more concerned about winning an ill-considered war in Vietnam than about winning the war against poverty here at home. It is disappointment with white legislators who pass laws in behalf of Negro rights that they never intended to implement. It is disappointment with the Christian church that appears to be more white than Christian, and with many white clergymen who prefer to remain silent behind the security of stained-glass windows. It is disappointment with some Negro clergymen who are more concerned about the size of the wheel base on their automobiles than about the quality of their service to the Negro community. It is disappointment with the Negro middle class that has sailed or struggled out of the muddy ponds into the relatively fresh-flowing waters of the mainstream, and in the process has forgotten the stench of the backwaters where their brothers are still drowning.

Second, Black Power, in its broad and positive meaning, is a call to black people to amass the political and economic strength to achieve their legitimate goals. No one can deny that the Negro is in dire need of this kind of legitimate power. Indeed, one of the great problems that the Negro confronts is his lack of power. From the old plantations of the South to the newer ghettos of the North, the Negro has been confined to a life of voicelessness and powerlessness. Stripped of the right to make decisions concerning his life and destiny, he has been subject to the authoritarian and sometimes whimsical decisions of the white power structure. The plantation and the ghetto were created by those who had power both to confine those who had no power and to perpetuate their powerlessness. The problem of transforming the ghetto is, therefore, a problem of power—a confrontation between the forces of power demanding change and the forces of power dedicated to preserving the status quo.

Power, properly understood, is the ability to achieve purpose. It is the strength required to bring about social, political or economic changes. In this sense power is not only desirable but necessary in order to implement the demands of love and justice. One of the greatest problems of history is that the concepts of love and power are usually contrasted as polar opposites. Love is identified with a resignation of power and power with a denial of love. It was this misinterpretation that caused Nietzsche, the philosopher of the "will to power," to reject the Christian concept of love. It was this same misinterpretation which induced Christian theologians to reject Nietzsche's philosophy of the "will to power" in the name of the Christian idea of love. What is needed is a realization that power without love is reckless and abusive and that love without power is sentimental and anemic. Power at its best is love implementing the demands of justice. Justice at its best is love correcting everything that stands against love.

There is nothing essentially wrong with power. The problem is that in America power is unequally distributed. This has led Negro Americans in the past to seek their goals through love and moral suasion devoid of power and white Americans to seek their goals through power devoid of love and conscience. It is leading a few extremists today to advocate for Negroes the same destructive and conscienceless power that they have justly abhorred in whites. It is precisely this collision of immoral power with powerless morality which constitutes the major crisis of our times.

In his struggle for racial justice, the Negro must seek to transform his condition of powerlessness into creative and positive power. One of the most obvious sources of this power is political. In *Why We Can't Wait*[3] I wrote at length of the need for Negroes to unite for political action in order to compel the majority to listen. I urged the development of political

[3] New York, Harper & Row, Publishers, 1964, pp. 162 ff.

awareness and strength in the Negro community, the election of blacks to key positions, and the use of the bloc vote to liberalize the political climate and achieve our just aspirations for freedom and human dignity. To the extent that Black Power advocates these goals, it is a positive and legitimate call to action that we in the civil rights movement have sought to follow all along and which we must intensify in the future.

Black Power is also a call for the pooling of black financial resources to achieve economic security. While the ultimate answer to the Negroes' economic dilemma will be found in a massive federal program for all the poor along the lines of A. Philip Randolph's Freedom Budget, a kind of Marshall Plan for the disadvantaged, there is something that the Negro himself can do to throw off the shackles of poverty. Although the Negro is still at the bottom of the economic ladder, his collective annual income is upwards of $30 billion. This gives him a considerable buying power that can make the difference between profit and loss in many businesses.

Through the pooling of such resources and the development of habits of thrift and techniques of wise investment, the Negro will be doing his share to grapple with his problem of economic deprivation. If Black Power means the development of this kind of strength within the Negro community, then it is a quest for basic, necessary, legitimate power.

Finally, Black Power is a psychological call to manhood. For years the Negro has been taught that he is nobody, that his color is a sign of his biological depravity, that his being has been stamped with an indelible imprint of inferiority, that his whole history has been soiled with the filth of worthlessness. All too few people realize how slavery and racial segregation have scarred the soul and wounded the spirit of the black man. The whole dirty business of slavery was based on the premise that the Negro was a thing to be used, not a person to be respected.

The historian Kenneth Stampp, in his remarkable book *The Peculiar Institution*,[4] has a fascinating section on the psychological indoctrination that was necessary from the mas-

---

[4] New York, Alfred A. Knopf, Inc., 1956, pp. 141–191.

ter's viewpoint to make a good slave. He gathered the material for this section primarily from the manuals and other documents which were produced by slaveowners on the subject of training slaves. Stampp notes five recurring aspects of this training.

First, those who managed the slaves had to maintain strict discipline. One master said, "Unconditional submission is the only footing upon which slavery should be placed." Another said, "The slave must know that his master is to govern absolutely and he is to obey implicitly, that he is never, for a moment, to exercise either his will or judgment in opposition to a positive order." Second, the masters felt that they had to implant in the bondsman a consciousness of personal inferiority. This sense of inferiority was deliberately extended to his past. The slaveowners were convinced that in order to control the Negroes, the slaves "had to feel that African ancestry tainted them, that their color was a badge of degradation." The third step in the training process was to awe the slaves with a sense of the masters' enormous power. It was necessary, various owners said, "to make them stand in fear." The fourth aspect was the attempt to "persuade the bondsman to take an interest in the master's enterprise and to accept his standards of good conduct." Thus the master's criteria of what was good and true and beautiful were to be accepted unquestioningly by the slaves. The final step, according to Stampp's documents, was "to impress Negroes with their helplessness: to create in them a habit of perfect dependence upon their masters."

Here, then, was the way to produce a perfect slave. Accustom him to rigid discipline, demand from him unconditional submission, impress upon him a sense of his innate inferiority, develop in him a paralyzing fear of white men, train him to adopt the master's code of good behavior, and instill in him a sense of complete dependence.

Out of the soil of slavery came the psychological roots of the Black Power cry. Anyone familiar with the Black Power movement recognizes that defiance of white authority and white power is a constant theme; the defiance almost becomes a kind of taunt. Underneath it, however, there is a legitimate concern that the Negro break away from "unconditional submission" and thereby assert his own selfhood.

Another obvious reaction of Black Power to the American system of slavery is the determination to glory in blackness and to resurrect joyously the African past. In response to the emphasis on their masters' "enormous power," Black Power advocates contend that the Negro must develop his own sense of strength. No longer are "fear, awe and obedience" to rule. This accounts for, though it does not justify, some Black Power advocates who encourage contempt and even uncivil disobedience as alternatives to the old patterns of slavery. Black Power assumes that Negroes will be slaves unless there is a new power to counter the force of the men who are still determined to be masters rather than brothers.

It is in the context of the slave tradition that some of the ideologues of the Black Power movement call for the need to develop new and indigenous codes of justice for the ghettos, so that blacks may move entirely away from their former masters' "standards of good conduct." Those in the Black Power movement who contend that blacks should cut themselves off from every level of dependence upon whites for advice, money or other help are obviously reacting against the slave pattern of "perfect dependence" upon the masters.

Black Power is a psychological reaction to the psychological indoctrination that led to the creation of the perfect slave. While this reaction has often led to negative and unrealistic responses and has frequently brought about intemperate words and actions, one must not overlook the positive value in calling the Negro to a new sense of manhood, to a deep feeling of racial pride and to an audacious appreciation of his heritage. The Negro must be grasped by a new realization of his dignity and worth. He must stand up amid a system that still oppresses him and develop an unassailable and majestic sense of his own value. He must no longer be ashamed of being black.

The job of arousing manhood within a people that have been taught for so many centuries that they are nobody is not easy. Even semantics have conspired to make that which is black seem ugly and degrading. In *Roget's Thesaurus* there are some 120 synonyms for "blackness" and at least 60 of them are offensive—such words as "blot," "soot," "grime," "devil" and "foul." There are some 134 synonyms for "whiteness," and all are favorable, expressed in such words as "purity," "cleanliness," "chastity" and "innocence." A white lie is better than a black lie. The most degenerate member of a family is the "black sheep," not the "white sheep." Ossie Davis has suggested that maybe the English language should be "reconstructed" so that teachers will not be forced to teach the Negro child 60 ways to despise himself and thereby perpetuate his false sense of inferiority and the white child 134 ways to adore himself and thereby perpetuate his false sense of superiority.

The history books, which have almost completely ignored the contribution of the Negro in American history, have only served to intensify the Negroes' sense of worthlessness and to augment the anachronistic doctrine of white supremacy. All too many Negroes and whites are unaware of the fact that the first American to shed blood in the revolution which freed this country from British oppression was a black seaman named Crispus Attucks. Negroes and whites are almost totally oblivious of the fact that it was a Negro physician, Dr. Daniel Hale Williams, who performed the first successful operation on the heart in America, and that another Negro physician, Dr. Charles Drew, was largely responsible for developing the method of separating blood plasma and storing it on a large scale, a process that saved thousands of lives in World War II and has made possible many of the important advances in postwar medicine. History books have virtually overlooked the many Negro scientists and inventors who have enriched American life. Although a few refer to George Washington Carver, whose research in agricultural products helped to revive the economy of the South when the throne of King Cotton began to totter, they ignore the contribution of Norbert Rillieux, whose invention of an evaporating pan revolutionized the process of sugar refining. How many people know that the multimillion-dollar United Shoe Machinery Company developed from the shoe-lasting machine invented in the last century by a Negro from Dutch Guiana, Jan Matzeliger; or that Granville T. Woods, an expert in electric motors, whose many patents speeded the growth and improvement of the railroads at the beginning of this century, was a Negro?

Even the Negroes' contribution to the music of America is sometimes overlooked in astonishing ways. Two years ago my oldest son and daughter entered an integrated school in Atlanta. A few months later my wife and I were invited to attend a program entitled "music that has made America great." As the evening unfolded, we listened to the folk songs and melodies of the various immigrant groups. We were certain that the program would end with the most original of all American music, the Negro spiritual. But we were mistaken. Instead, all the students, including our children, ended the program by singing "Dixie."

As we rose to leave the hall, my wife and I looked at each other with a combination of indignation and amazement. All the students, black and white, all the parents present that night, and all the faculty members had been victimized by just another expression of America's penchant for ignoring the Negro, making him invisible and making his contributions insignificant. I wept within that night. I wept for my children and all black children who have been denied a knowledge of their heritage; I wept for all white children, who, through daily miseducation, are taught that the Negro is an irrelevant entity in American society; I wept for all the white parents and teachers who are forced to overlook the fact that the wealth of cultural and technological progress in America is a result of the commonwealth of inpouring contributions.

The tendency to ignore the Negro's contribution to American life and strip him of his personhood is as old as the earliest history books and as contemporary as the morning's newspaper. To offset this cultural homicide, the Negro must rise up with an affirmation of his own Olympian manhood. Any movement for the Negro's freedom that overlooks this necessity is only waiting to be buried. As long as the mind is enslaved the body can never be free. Psychological freedom, a firm sense of self-esteem, is the most powerful weapon against the long night of physical slavery. No Lincolnian Emancipation Proclamation or Kennedyan or Johnsonian civil rights bill can totally bring this kind of freedom. The Negro will only be truly free when he reaches down to the inner depths of his own being and signs with the pen and ink of assertive selfhood his own emancipation proclamation. With a spirit straining toward true self-esteem, the Negro must boldly throw off the manacles of self-abnegation and say to himself and the world: "I am somebody. I am a person. I am a man with dignity and honor. I have a rich and noble history, however painful and exploited that history has been. I am black *and* comely." This self-affirmation is the black man's need made compelling by the white man's crimes against him. This is positive and necessary power for black people.

### III

Nevertheless, in spite of the positive aspects of Black Power, which are compatible with what we have sought to do in the civil rights movement all along without the slogan, its negative values, I believe, prevent it from having the substance and program to become the basic strategy for the civil rights movement in the days ahead.

Beneath all the satisfaction of a gratifying slogan, Black Power is a nihilistic philosophy born out of the conviction that the Negro can't win. It is, at bottom, the view that American society is so hopelessly corrupt and enmeshed in evil that there is no possibility of salvation from within. Although this thinking is understandable as a response to a white power structure that never completely committed itself to true equality for the Negro, and a die-hard mentality that sought to shut all windows and doors against the winds of change, it nonetheless carries the seeds of its own doom.

Before this century, virtually all revolutions had been based on hope and hate. The hope was expressed in the rising expectation of freedom and justice. The hate was an expression of bitterness toward the perpetrators of the old order. It was the hate that made revolutions bloody and violent. What was new about Mahatma Gandhi's movement in India was that he mounted a revolution on hope and love, hope and nonviolence. This same new emphasis characterized the civil rights movement in our country dating from the Montgomery bus boycott of 1956 to the Selma movement of 1965. We maintained the hope while transforming the hate of traditional revolution into positive nonviolent power. As long as the hope was fulfilled there was little questioning of nonviolence. But when the hopes were blasted, when people came to see that in spite of progress their conditions were still insufferable, when they looked out and saw more poverty, more school segregation and more slums, despair began to set in.

Unfortunately, when hope diminishes, the hate is often turned most bitterly toward those who originally built up the hope. In all the speaking that I have done in the United States before varied audiences, including some hostile whites, the only time that I have been booed was one night in a Chicago mass meeting by some young members of the Black Power movement. I went home that night with an ugly feeling. Selfishly I thought of my sufferings and sacrifices over the last twelve years. Why would they boo one so close to them? But as I lay awake thinking, I finally came to myself, and I could not for the life of me have less than patience and understanding for those young people. For twelve years I, and others like me, had held out radiant promises of progress. I had preached to them about my dream. I had lectured to them about the not too distant day when they would have freedom, "all, here and now." I had urged them to have faith in America and in white society. Their hopes had soared. They were now booing because they felt that we were unable to deliver on our promises. They were booing because we had urged them to have faith in people who had too often proved to be unfaithful. They were now hostile because they were watching the dream that they had so readily accepted turn into a frustrating nightmare.

But revolution, though born of despair, cannot long be sustained by despair. This is the ultimate contradiction of the Black Power movement. It claims to be the most revolutionary wing of the social revolution taking place in the United

States. Yet it rejects the one thing that keeps the fire of revolutions burning: the ever-present flame of hope. When hope dies, a revolution degenerates into an undiscriminating catchall for evanescent and futile gestures. The Negro cannot entrust his destiny to a philosophy nourished solely on despair, to a slogan that cannot be implemented into a program.

The Negro's disappointment is real and a part of the daily menu of our lives. One of the most agonizing problems of human experience is how to deal with disappointment. In our individual lives we all too often distill our frustrations into an essence of bitterness, or drown ourselves in the deep waters of self-pity, or adopt a fatalistic philosophy that whatever happens must happen and all events are determined by necessity. These reactions poison the soul and scar the personality, always harming the person who harbors them more than anyone else. The only healthy answer lies in one's honest recognition of disappointment even as he still clings to hope, one's acceptance of finite disappointment even while clinging to infinite hope.

We Negroes, who have dreamed for so long of freedom, are still confined in a prison of segregation and discrimination. Must we respond with bitterness and cynicism? Certainly not, for this can lead to black anger so desperate that it ends in black suicide. Must we turn inward in self-pity? Of course not, for this can lead to a self-defeating black paranoia. Must we conclude that we cannot win? Certainly not, for this will lead to a black nihilism that seeks disruption for disruption's sake. Must we, by fatalistically concluding that segregation is a foreordained pattern of the universe, resign ourselves to oppression? Of course not, for passively to cooperate with an unjust system makes the oppressed as evil as the oppressors. Our most fruitful course is to stand firm, move forward nonviolently, accept disappointments and cling to hope. Our determined refusal not to be stopped will eventually open the door to fulfillment. By recognizing the necessity of suffering in a righteous cause, we may achieve our humanity's full stature. To guard ourselves from bitterness, we need the vision to see in this generation's ordeals the opportunity to trans-figure both ourselves and American society.

In 1956 I flew from New York to London in the propeller-type aircraft that required nine and a half hours for a flight now made in six hours by jet. Returning from London to the United States, the stewardess announced that the flying time would be twelve and a half hours. The distance was the same. Why an additional three hours? When the pilot entered the cabin to greet the passengers, I asked him to explain.

"You must understand about the winds," he said. "When we leave New York, a strong tail wind is in our favor, but when we return, a strong head wind is against us." Then he added, "Don't worry. These four engines are capable of battling the winds."

In any social revolution there are times when the tail winds of triumph and fulfillment favor us, and other times when strong head winds of disappointment and setbacks beat against us relentlessly. We must not permit adverse winds to over-whelm us as we journey across life's mighty Atlantic; we must be sustained by our engines of courage in spite of the winds. This refusal to be stopped, this "courage to be," this determination to go on "in spite of" is the hallmark of any great movement.

The Black Power movement of today, like the Garvey "Back to Africa" movement of the 1920's, represents a dashing of hope, a conviction of the inability of the Negro to win and a belief in the infinitude of the ghetto. While there is much grounding in past experience for all these feelings, a revolution cannot succumb to any of them. Today's despair is a poor chisel to carve out tomorrow's justice.

Black Power is an implicit and often explicit belief in black separatism. Notice that I do not call it black racism. It is inaccurate to refer to Black Power as racism in reverse, as some have recently done. Racism is a doctrine of the con-genital inferiority and worthlessness of a people. While a few angry proponents of Black Power have, in moments of bitterness, made wild statements that come close to this kind of racism, the major proponents of Black Power have never contended that the white man is innately worthless.

Yet behind Black Power's legitimate and necessary concern for group unity and black identity lies the belief that there can be a separate black road to power and fulfillment. Few ideas are more unrealistic. There is no salvation for the Negro through isolation.

One of the chief affirmations of Black Power is the call for the mobilization of political strength for black people. But we do not have to look far to see that effective political power for Negroes cannot come through separatism. Granted that there are cities and counties in the country where the Negro is in a majority, they are so few that concentration on them alone would still leave the vast majority of Negroes outside the mainstream of American political life.

Out of the eighty-odd counties in Alabama, the state where SNCC sought to develop an all-black party, only nine have a majority of Negroes. Even if blacks could control each of these counties, they would have little influence in over-all state politics and could do little to improve conditions in the major Negro population centers of Birmingham, Mobile and Montgomery. There are still relatively few Congressional districts in the South that have such large black majorities that Negro candidates could be elected without the aid of whites. Is it a sounder program to concentrate on the election of two or three Negro Congressmen from predominantly Negro districts or to concentrate on the election of fifteen or twenty Negro Congressmen from Southern districts where a coalition of Negro and white moderate voters is possible?

Moreover, any program that elects all black candidates simply because they are black and rejects all white candidates simply because they are white is politically unsound and morally unjustifiable. It is true that in many areas of the South Negroes still must elect Negroes in order to be effectively represented. SNCC staff members are eminently correct when they point out that in Lowndes County, Alabama, there are no white liberals or moderates and no possibility for cooperation between the races at the present time. But the Lowndes County experience cannot be made a measuring rod for the whole of America. The basic thing in determining the best candidate is not his color but his integrity.

Black Power alone is no more insurance against social injustice than white power. Negro politicians can be as opportunistic as their white counterparts if there is not an informed and determined constituency demanding social reform. What is most needed is a coalition of Negroes and liberal whites that will work to make both major parties truly responsive to the needs of the poor. Black Power does not envision or desire such a program.

Just as the Negro cannot achieve political power in isolation, neither can he gain economic power through separatism. While there must be a continued emphasis on the need for blacks to pool their economic resources and withdraw consumer support from discriminating firms, we must not be oblivious to the fact that the larger economic problems confronting the Negro community will only be solved by federal programs involving billions of dollars. One unfortunate thing about Black Power is that it gives priority to race precisely at a time when the impact of automation and other forces have made the economic question fundamental for blacks and whites alike. In this context a slogan Power for Poor People would be much more appropriate than the slogan Black Power.

However much we pool our resources and "buy black," this cannot create the multiplicity of new jobs and provide the number of low-cost houses that will lift the Negro out of the economic depression caused by centuries of deprivation. Neither can our resources supply quality integrated education. All of this requires billions of dollars which only an alliance of liberal-labor-civil-rights forces can stimulate. In short, the Negroes' problem cannot be solved unless the whole of American society takes a new turn toward greater economic justice.

In a multiracial society no group can make it alone. It is a myth to believe that the Irish, the Italians and the Jews— the ethnic groups that Black Power advocates cite as justification for their views—rose to power through separatism. It is true that they stuck together. But their group unity was always enlarged by joining in alliances with other groups such as political machines and trade unions. To succeed in a pluralistic society, and an often hostile one at that, the Negro obviously needs organized strength, but that strength will only be effective when it is consolidated through constructive alliances with the majority group.

Those proponents of Black Power who have urged Negroes to shun alliances with whites argue that whites as a group cannot have a genuine concern for Negro progress. Therefore, they claim, the white man's main interest in collaborative effort is to diminish Negro militancy and deflect it from constructive goals.

Undeniably there are white elements that cannot be trusted, and no militant movement can afford to relax its vigilance against halfhearted associates or conscious betrayers. Every alliance must be considered on its own merits. Negroes may embrace some and walk out on others where their interests are imperiled. Occasional betrayals, however, do not justify the rejection of the principle of Negro-white alliance.

The oppression of Negroes by whites has left an understandable residue of suspicion. Some of this suspicion is a healthy and appropriate safeguard. An excess of skepticism, however, becomes a fetter. It denies that there can be reliable white allies, even though some whites have died heroically at the side of Negroes in our struggle and others have risked economic and political peril to support our cause.

The history of the movement reveals that Negro-white alliances have played a powerfully constructive role, especially in recent years. While Negro initiative, courage and imagination precipitated the Birmingham and Selma confrontations and revealed the harrowing injustice of segregated life, the organized strength of Negroes alone would have been insufficient to move Congress and the administration without the weight of the aroused conscience of white America. In the period ahead Negroes will continue to need this support. Ten percent of the population cannot by tensions alone induce 90 percent to change a way of life.

Within the white majority there exists a substantial group

who cherish democratic principles above privilege and who have demonstrated a will to fight side by side with the Negro against injustice. Another and more substantial group is composed of those having common needs with the Negro and who will benefit equally with him in the achievement of social progress. There are, in fact, more poor white Americans than there are Negro. Their need for a war on poverty is no less desperate than the Negro's. In the South they have been deluded by race prejudice and largely remained aloof from common action. Ironically, with this posture they were fighting not only the Negro but themselves. Yet there are already signs of change. Without formal alliances, Negroes and whites have supported the same candidates in many *de facto* electoral coalitions in the South because each sufficiently served his own needs.

The ability of Negroes to enter alliances is a mark of our growing strength, not of our weakness. In entering an alliance, the Negro is not relying on white leadership or ideology; he is taking his place as an equal partner in a common endeavor. His organized strength and his new independence pave the way for alliances. Far from losing independence in an alliance, he is using it for constructive and multiplied gains.

Negroes must shun the very narrow-mindedness that in others has so long been the source of our own afflictions. We have reached the stage of organized strength and independence to work securely in alliances. History has demonstrated with major victories the effectiveness, wisdom and moral soundness of Negro-white alliance. The cooperation of Negro and white based on the solid ground of honest conscience and proper self-interest can continue to grow in scope and influence. It can attain the strength to alter basic institutions by democratic means. Negro isolation can never approach this goal.

In the final analysis the weakness of Black Power is its failure to see that the black man needs the white man and the white man needs the black man. However much we may try to romanticize the slogan, there is no separate black path to power and fulfillment that does not intersect white paths, and there is no separate white path to power and fulfillment, short of social disaster, that does not share that power with black aspirations for freedom and human dignity. We are bound together in a single garment of destiny. The language, the cultural patterns, the music, the material prosperity and even the food of America are an amalgam of black and white.

James Baldwin once related how he returned home from school and his mother asked him whether his teacher was colored or white. After a pause he answered: "She is a little bit colored and a little bit white."[5] This is the dilemma of being a Negro in America. In physical as well as cultural terms every Negro is a little bit colored and a little bit white. In our search for identity we must recognize this dilemma.

Every man must ultimately confront the question "Who am I?" and seek to answer it honestly. One of the first principles of personal adjustment is the principle of self-acceptance. The Negro's greatest dilemma is that in order to be healthy he must accept his ambivalence. The Negro is the child of two cultures— Africa and America. The problem is that in the search for wholeness all too many Negroes seek to embrace only one side of their natures. Some, seeking to reject their heritage, are ashamed of their color, ashamed of black art and music, and determine what is beautiful and good by the standards of white society. They end up frustrated and without cultural roots. Others seek to reject everything American and to identify totally with Africa, even to the point of wearing African clothes. But this approach leads also to frustration because the American Negro is not an African. The old Hegelian synthesis still offers the best answer to many of life's dilemmas. The American Negro is neither totally African nor totally Western. He is Afro-American, a true hybrid, a combination of two cultures.

Who are we? We are the descendants of slaves. We are the offspring of noble men and women who were kidnaped from their native land and chained in ships like beasts. We are the heirs of a great and exploited continent known as Africa. We are the heirs of a past of rope, fire and murder. I for one am

[5] Quoted in Kenneth B. Clark (ed.), *The Negro Protest*, Boston, Beacon Press, 1963, p. 6.

not ashamed of this past. My shame is for those who became so inhuman that they could inflict this torture upon us.

But we are also Americans. Abused and scorned though we may be, our destiny is tied up with the destiny of America. In spite of the psychological appeals of identification with Africa, the Negro must face the fact that America is now his home, a home that he helped to build through "blood, sweat and tears." Since we are Americans the solution to our problem will not come through seeking to build a separate black nation within a nation, but by finding that creative minority of the concerned from the ofttimes apathetic majority, and together moving toward that colorless power that we all need for security and justice.

In the first century B.C., Cicero said: "Freedom is participation in power." Negroes should never want all power because they would deprive others of their freedom. By the same token, Negroes can never be content without participation in power. America must be a nation in which its multiracial people are partners in power. This is the essence of democracy toward which all Negro struggles have been directed since the distant past when he was transplanted here in chains.

Probably the most destructive feature of Black Power is its unconscious and often conscious call for retaliatory violence. Many well-meaning persons within the movement rationalize that Black Power does not really mean black violence, that those who shout the slogan don't really mean it that way, that the violent connotations are solely the distortions of a vicious press. That the press has fueled the fire is true. But as one who has worked and talked intimately with devotees of Black Power, I must admit that the slogan is mainly used by persons who have lost faith in the method and philosophy of nonviolence. I must make it clear that no guilt by association is intended. Both Floyd McKissick and Stokely Carmichael have declared themselves opponents of aggressive violence. This clarification is welcome and useful, despite the persistence of some of their followers in examining the uses of violence.

Over cups of coffee in my home in Atlanta and my apartment in Chicago, I have often talked late at night and over into the small hours of the morning with proponents of Black Power who argued passionately about the validity of violence and riots. They don't quote Gandhi or Tolstoy. Their Bible is Frantz Fanon's *The Wretched of the Earth*.[6] This black psychiatrist from Martinique, who went to Algeria to work with the National Liberation Front in its fight against the French, argues in his book—a well-written book, incidentally, with many penetrating insights—that violence is a psychologically healthy and tactically sound method for the oppressed. And so, realizing that they are a part of that vast company of the "wretched of the earth," these young American Negroes, who are predominantly involved in the Black Power movement, often quote Fanon's belief that violence is the only thing that will bring about liberation. As they say, "Sing us no songs of nonviolence, sing us no songs of progress, for nonviolence and progress belong to middle-class Negroes and whites and we are not interested in you."

As we have seen, the first public expression of disenchantment with nonviolence arose around the question of "self-defense." In a sense this is a false issue, for the right to defend one's home and one's person when attacked has been guaranteed through the ages by common law. In a nonviolent demonstration, however, self-defense must be approached from another perspective.

The cause of a demonstration is the existence of some form of exploitation or oppression that has made it necessary for men of courage and goodwill to protest the evil. For example, a demonstration against *de facto* school segregation is based on the awareness that a child's mind is crippled by inadequate educational opportunities. The demonstrator agrees that it is better to suffer publicly for a short time to end the crippling evil of school segregation than to have generation after generation of children suffer in ignorance. In such a demonstration the point is made that the schools are inadequate. This is the evil one seeks to dramatize; anything else distracts from that point and interferes with the confrontation of the

6 New York, Evergreen Books, Grove Press, Inc., 1966.

primary evil. Of course no one wants to suffer and be hurt. But it is more important to get at the cause than to be safe. It is better to shed a little blood from a blow on the head or a rock thrown by an angry mob than to have children by the thousands finishing high school who can only read at a sixth-grade level.

Furthermore, it is dangerous to organize a movement around self-defense. The line of demarcation between defensive violence and aggressive violence is very thin. The minute a program of violence is enunciated, even for self-defense, the atmosphere is filled with talk of violence, and the words falling on unsophisticated ears may be interpreted as an invitation to aggression.

One of the main questions that the Negro must confront in his pursuit of freedom is that of effectiveness. What is the most effective way to achieve the desired goal? If a method is not effective, no matter how much steam it releases, it is an expression of weakness, not of strength. Now the plain, inexorable fact is that any attempt of the American Negro to overthrow his oppressor with violence will not work. We do not need President Johnson to tell us this by reminding Negro rioters that they are outnumbered ten to one. The courageous efforts of our own insurrectionist brothers, such as Denmark Vesey and Nat Turner, should be eternal reminders to us that violent rebellion is doomed from the start. In violent warfare one must be prepared to face the fact that there will be casualties by the thousands. Anyone leading a violent rebellion must be willing to make an honest assessment regarding the possible casualties to a minority population confronting a well-armed, wealthy majority with a fanatical right wing that would delight in exterminating thousands of black men, women and children.

Arguments that the American Negro is a part of a world which is two-thirds colored and that there will come a day when the oppressed people of color will violently rise together to throw off the yoke of white oppression are beyond the realm of serious discussion. There is no colored nation, including China, that now shows even the potential of leading a violent revolution of color in any international proportions. Ghana, Zambia, Tanganyika and Nigeria are so busy fighting their own battles against poverty, illiteracy and the subversive influence of neo-colonialism that they offer little hope to Angola, Southern Rhodesia and South Africa, much less to the American Negro. The hard cold facts today indicate that the hope of the people of color in the world may well rest on the American Negro and his ability to reform the structure of racist imperialism from within and thereby turn the technology and wealth of the West to the task of liberating the world from want.

The futility of violence in the struggle for racial justice has been tragically etched in all the recent Negro riots. There is something painfully sad about a riot. One sees screaming youngsters and angry adults fighting hopelessly and aimlessly against impossible odds. Deep down within them you perceive a desire for self-destruction, a suicidal longing. Occasionally Negroes contend that the 1965 Watts riot and the other riots in various cities represented effective civil rights action. But those who express this view always end up with stumbling words when asked what concrete gains have been won as a result. At best the riots have produced a little additional anti-poverty money, allotted by frightened government officials, and a few water sprinklers to cool the children of the ghettos. It is something like improving the food in a prison while the people remain securely incarcerated behind bars. Nowhere have the riots won any concrete improvement such as have the organized protest demonstrations.

It is not overlooking the limitations of nonviolence and the distance we have yet to go to point out the remarkable record of achievements that have already come through nonviolent action. The 1960 sit-ins desegregated lunch counters in more than 150 cities within a year. The 1961 Freedom Rides put an end to segregation in interstate travel. The 1956 bus boycott in Montgomery, Alabama, ended segregation on the buses not only of that city but in practically every city of the South. The 1963 Birmingham movement and the climactic March on Washington won passage of the most powerful civil rights law in a century. The 1965 Selma movement brought enactment of the Voting Rights Law. Our nonviolent marches in Chicago last summer brought about a housing agreement which, if implemented, will be the strongest step toward open housing taken in any city in the nation. Most significant is the fact that this progress occurred with minimum human sacrifice and loss of life. Fewer people have been killed in ten years of nonviolent demonstrations across the South than were killed in one night of rioting in Watts.

When one tries to pin down advocates of violence as to what acts would be effective, the answers are blatantly illogical. Sometimes they talk of overthrowing racist state and local governments. They fail to see that no internal revolution has ever succeeded in overthrowing a government by violence unless the government had already lost the allegiance and effective control of its armed forces. Anyone in his right mind knows that this will not happen in the United States. In a violent racial situation, the power structure has the local police, the state troopers, the national guard and finally the army to call on, all of which are predominantly white.

Furthermore, few if any violent revolutions have been successful unless the violent minority had the sympathy and support of the nonresisting majority. Castro may have had only a few Cubans actually fighting with him, but he would never have overthrown the Batista regime unless he had had the sympathy of the vast majority of the Cuban people. It is perfectly clear that a violent revolution on the part of American blacks would find no sympathy and support from the white population and very little from the majority of the Negroes themselves.

This is no time for romantic illusions and empty philosophical debates about freedom. This is a time for action. What is needed is a strategy for change, a tactical program that will bring the Negro into the mainstream of American life as quickly as possible. So far, this has only been offered by the nonviolent movement. Without recognizing this we will end up with solutions that don't solve, answers that don't answer and explanations that don't explain.

Beyond the pragmatic invalidity of violence is its inability to appeal to conscience. Some Black Power advocates consider an appeal to conscience irrelevant. A Black Power exponent said to me not long ago: "To hell' with conscience and morality. We want power." But power and morality must go together, implementing, fulfilling and ennobling each other. In the quest for power I cannot by-pass the concern for morality. I refuse to be driven to a Machiavellian cynicism with respect to power. Power at its best is the right use of strength. The words of Alfred the Great are still true: "Power is never good unless he who has it is good."

Nonviolence is power, but it is the right and good use of power. Constructively it can save the white man as well as the Negro. Racial segregation is buttressed by such irrational fears as loss of preferred economic privilege, altered social status, intermarriage and adjustment to new situations. Through sleepless nights and haggard days numerous white people struggle pitifully to combat these fears. By following the path of escape, some seek to ignore the questions of race relations and to close their minds to the issues involved. Others, placing their faith in legal maneuvers, counsel massive resistance. Still others hope to drown their fears by engaging in acts of meanness and violence toward their Negro brethren. But how futile are all these remedies! Instead of eliminating fear, they instill deeper and more pathological fears. The white man, through his own efforts, through education and goodwill, through searching his conscience and through confronting the fact of integration, must do a great deal to free himself of these paralyzing fears. But to master fear he must also depend on the spirit the Negro generates toward him. Only through our adherence to nonviolence—which also means love in its strong and commanding sense—will the fear in the white community be mitigated.

A guilt-ridden white minority fears that if the Negro attains power, he will without restraint or pity act to revenge the accumulated injustices and brutality of the years. The Negro must show that the white man has nothing to fear, for the Negro is willing to forgive. A mass movement exercising nonviolence and demonstrating power under discipline should convince the white community that as such a movement attained strength, its power would be used creatively and not for revenge.

In a moving letter to his nephew on the one hundredth

anniversary of emancipation, James Baldwin wrote concerning white people:

> The really terrible thing, old buddy, is that *you* must accept *them*. And I mean that very seriously. You must accept them and accept them with love. For these innocent people have no other hope. They are, in effect, still trapped in a history which they do not understand; and until they understand it, they cannot be released from it. They have had to believe for many years, and for innumerable reasons, that black men are inferior to white men. Many of them, indeed, know better, but, as you will discover, people find it very difficult to act on what they know. To act is to be committed, and to be committed is to be in danger. In this case, the danger, in the minds of most white Americans, is the loss of their identity. . . . But these men are your brothers—your lost, younger brothers. And if the word *integration* means anything, this is what it means: that we, with love, shall force our brothers to see themselves as they are, to cease fleeing from reality and begin to change it. . . .[7]

The problem with hatred and violence is that they intensify the fears of the white majority, and leave them less ashamed of their prejudices toward Negroes. In the guilt and confusion confronting our society, violence only adds to the chaos. It deepens the brutality of the oppressor and increases the bitterness of the oppressed. Violence is the antithesis of creativity and wholeness. It destroys community and makes brotherhood impossible.

My friend John Killens recently wrote in the *Negro Digest:*

> Integration comes after liberation. A slave cannot integrate with his master. In the whole history of revolts and revolutions, integration has never been the main slogan of the revolution. The oppressed fights to free himself from

---

[7] *The Fire Next Time*, New York, The Dial Press, Inc., 1963, pp. 22–23.

his oppressor, not to integrate with him. Integration is
the step after freedom when the freedman makes up his
mind as to whether he wishes to integrate with his former
master.[8]

At first glance this sounds very good. But after reflection
one has to face some inescapable facts about the Negro and
American life. This is a multiracial nation where all groups
are dependent on each other, whether they want to recognize
it or not. In this vast interdependent nation no racial group
can retreat to an island entire of itself. The phenomena of integration and liberation cannot be as neatly divided as Killens
would have it.

There is no theoretical or sociological divorce between liberation and integration. In our kind of society liberation cannot
come without integration and integration cannot come without
liberation. I speak here of integration in both the ethical and
the political senses. On the one hand, integration is true inter-
group, interpersonal living. On the other hand, it is the mutual
sharing of power. I cannot see how the Negro will be totally
liberated from the crushing weight of poor education, squalid
housing and economic strangulation until he is integrated, with
power, into every level of American life.

Mr. Killens' assertion might have some validity in a struggle
for independence against a foreign invader. But the Negro's
struggle in America is quite different from and more difficult
than the struggle for independence. The American Negro will
be living tomorrow with the very people against whom he is
struggling today. The American Negro is not in a Congo where
the Belgians will go back to Belgium after the battle is over,
or in an India where the British will go back to England after
independence is won. In the struggle for national independence
one can talk about liberation now and integration later, but in
the struggle for racial justice in a multiracial society where the
oppressor and the oppressed are both "at home," liberation must
come through integration.

[8] *Negro Digest*, November, 1966.

Are we seeking power for power's sake? Or are we seeking to make the world and our nation better places to live. If we seek the latter, violence can never provide the answer. The ultimate weakness of violence is that it is a descending spiral, begetting the very thing it seeks to destroy. Instead of diminishing evil, it multiplies it. Through violence you may murder the liar, but you cannot murder the lie, nor establish the truth. Through violence you may murder the hater, but you do not murder hate. In fact, violence merely increases hate. So it goes. Returning violence for violence multiplies violence, adding deeper darkness to a night already devoid of stars. Darkness cannot drive out darkness: only light can do that. Hate cannot drive out hate: only love can do that.

The beauty of nonviolence is that in its own way and in its own time it seeks to break the chain reaction of evil. With a majestic sense of spiritual power, it seeks to elevate truth, beauty and goodness to the throne. Therefore I will continue to follow this method because I think it is the most practically sound and morally excellent way for the Negro to achieve freedom.

## IV

In recent months several people have said to me: "Since violence is the new cry, isn't there a danger that you will lose touch with the people in the ghetto and be out of step with the times if you don't change your views on nonviolence?"

My answer is always the same. While I am convinced the vast majority of Negroes reject violence, even if they did not I would not be interested in being a consensus leader. I refuse to determine what is right by taking a Gallup poll of the trends of the time. I imagine that there were leaders in Germany who sincerely opposed what Hitler was doing to the Jews. But they took their poll and discovered that anti-Semitism was the prevailing trend. In order to "be in step with the times," in order to "keep in touch," they yielded to one of the most ignominious evils that history has ever known.

Ultimately a genuine leader is not a searcher for consensus

but a molder of consensus. I said on one occasion, "If every Negro in the United States turns to violence, I will choose to be that one lone voice preaching that this is the wrong way." Maybe this sounded like arrogance. But it was not intended that way. It was simply my way of saying that I would rather be a man of conviction than a man of conformity. Occasionally in life one develops a conviction so precious and meaningful that he will stand on it till the end. This is what I have found in nonviolence.

One of the greatest paradoxes of the Black Power movement is that it talks unceasingly about not imitating the values of white society, but in advocating violence it is imitating the worst, the most brutal and the most uncivilized value of American life. American Negroes have not been mass murderers. They have not murdered children in Sunday school, nor have they hung white men on trees bearing strange fruit. They have not been hooded perpetrators of violence, lynching human beings at will and drowning them at whim.

This is not to imply that the Negro is a saint who abhors violence. Unfortunately, a check of the hospitals in any Negro community on any Saturday night will make you painfully aware of the violence within the Negro community. By turning his hostility and frustration with the larger society inward, the Negro often inflicts terrible acts of violence on his own black brother. This tragic problem must be solved. But I would not advise Negroes to solve the problem by turning these inner hostilities outward through the murdering of whites. This would substitute one evil for another. Nonviolence provides a healthy way to deal with understandable anger.

I am concerned that Negroes achieve full status as citizens and as human beings here in the United States. But I am also concerned about our moral uprightness and the health of our souls. Therefore I must oppose any attempt to gain our freedom by the methods of malice, hate and violence that have characterized our oppressors. Hate is just as injurious to the hater as it is to the hated. Like an unchecked cancer, hate corrodes the personality and eats away its vital unity. Many of our inner conflicts are rooted in hate. This is why the psychiatrists say, "Love or perish." I have seen hate expressed in the countenances of too many Mississippi and Alabama sheriffs to advise the Negro to sink to this miserable level. Hate is too great a burden to bear.

Of course, you may say, this is not *practical;* life is a matter of getting even, of hitting back, of dog eat dog. Maybe in some distant Utopia, you say, that idea will work, but not in the hard, cold world in which we live. My only answer is that mankind has followed the so-called practical way for a long time now, and it has led inexorably to deeper confusion and chaos. Time is cluttered with the wreckage of individuals and communities that surrendered to hatred and violence. For the salvation of our nation and the salvation of mankind, we must follow another way. This does not mean that we abandon our militant efforts. With every ounce of our energy we must continue to rid our nation of the incubus of racial injustice. But we need not in the process relinquish our privilege and obligation to love.

Fanon says at the end of *The Wretched of the Earth:*

> So, comrades, let us not pay tribute to Europe by creating states, institutions and societies which draw their inspiration from her.
>
> Humanity is waiting for something other from us than such an imitation, which would be almost an obscene caricature.
>
> If we want to turn Africa into a new Europe, and America into a new Europe, then let us leave the destiny of our countries to Europeans. They will know how to do it better than the most gifted among us.
>
> But if we want humanity to advance a step further, if we want to bring it up to a different level than that which Europe has shown it, then we must invent and we must make discoveries.
>
> If we wish to live up to our peoples' expectations, we must seek the response elsewhere than in Europe.
>
> Moreover, if we wish to reply to the expectations of the people of Europe, it is no good sending them back a

reflection, even an ideal reflection, of their society and their thought with which from time to time they feel immeasurably sickened.

For Europe, for ourselves and for humanity, comrades, we must turn over a new leaf, we must work out new concepts, and try to set afoot a new man.[9]

These are brave and challenging words; I am happy that young black men and women are quoting them. But the problem is that Fanon and those who quote his words are seeking "to work out new concepts" and "set afoot a new man" with a willingness to imitate old concepts of violence. Is there not a basic contradiction here? Violence has been the inseparable twin of materialism, the hallmark of its grandeur and misery. This is the one thing about modern civilization that I do not care to imitate.

Humanity is waiting for something other than blind imitation of the past. If we want truly to advance a step further, if we want to turn over a new leaf and really set a new man afoot, we must begin to turn mankind away from the long and desolate night of violence. May it not be that the new man the world needs is the nonviolent man? Longfellow said, "In this world a man must either be an anvil or a hammer." We must be hammers shaping a new society rather than anvils molded by the old. This not only will make us new men, but will give us a new kind of power. It will not be Lord Acton's image of power that tends to corrupt or absolute power that corrupts absolutely. It will be power infused with love and justice, that will change dark yesterdays into bright tomorrows, and lift us from the fatigue of despair to the buoyancy of hope. A dark, desperate, confused and sin-sick world waits for this new kind of man and this new kind of power.

[9] Fanon, *op. cit.*, p. 255.

## CHAPTER FOUR

# Address at the NAACP Convention, July 6, 1966

*Hubert H. Humphrey*

Before Hubert H. Humphrey, Vice President of the United States, took the platform in Los Angeles, the nation's attention had been riveted on the issue of Black Power. The day before, Roy Wilkins, President of the NAACP, had taken a clear stand against the implications of the slogan. It would have been difficult for the Vice President to have avoided the issue; even silence would have been interpreted as significant by hundreds of reporters.

After reading our criticism of his speech (which constitutes Chapter Five of this book), Mr. Humphrey explained his purpose in a letter to us:

> My purpose in the NAACP Convention speech was to emphasize the importance of responsible Negro leadership as a means of maintaining a broad base coalition of white and black to promote racial equality and justice. At the same time, I wanted to emphasize the tremendous amount of work left to do in the civil rights struggle.
>
> I wanted to repudiate all forms of racism—white power, black power, or whatever power that tends to be more divisive than cohesive.
>
> I wanted to strengthen the hands of those who have fought the good fight for years.
>
> Thus, rather than trying to interpret black power so as to make it acceptable as a symbol, I sought to speak of leadership committed to real progress, of greater integration, not segregation, of the power of all the people to do what is right and what they can to promote civil rights in the country. These are the things I wanted to project. The immediate audience and the national audience were most receptive to it.

SOURCE: This address is reprinted from the *Congressional Record* (July 12, 1966, pp. A3607–A3609).

America is marching on the road to freedom.

I am proud to be back among my friends of the NAACP who have led this march for 57 years.

From the shadows of a dark past toward the shining hope of a brighter tomorrow, this march has been difficult, uncertain, and often dangerous. But history shall surely record its glory.

For we marched . . . even when our band was small and our ranks thin and ragged . . . even when victory seemed a distant and unattainable goal.

There have been young marchers and old . . . Negro and white . . . rich and poor . . . but always marching with a common spirit—moved by a common hope—and striving for a common objective.

We marched and fought against separate and unequal education, and segregated lunch counters, and a seat in the back of the bus.

There have been defeats, but many more victories.

There have been many heroes, and some martyrs.

Yes, the road to freedom is stained with tears and the blood of many Americans—including men such as Medgar Evers—men already counted among authentic American heroes.

We have learned there is no single road to follow . . . no one program . . . no one slogan that will bring us to the end of our march.

There have been many things to do, and many roles to play. And through the years the NAACP has played a role second to none in terms of dedication and determination of sacrifice and courage.

We are here today because of millions of hours spent in the courthouse and on the courthouse steps—sitting down and standing up—in voter registration drives and in the halls of Congress.

Our triumphs have been impressive and numerous. Our progress has been unmistakable. Yet these triumphs and this progress must be judged from the perspective of the man who has borne the burden of oppression and prejudice.

A generation ago, it may have been enough for the Negro to ask for the right to enter a restaurant.

But today the Negro American asks:

Is my life better? Are my children attending better schools? Do I hold a better job—or any job? Do I have a voice in the life of my city and my neighborhood? Am I a first-class citizen —a man among men, in my own eyes and in the eyes of my family?

Until a man can truthfully answer "yes" to these questions, we should not expect him to consider the battle won or the struggle ended. And neither should we.

For what is left for such a man when the dust of the march has settled?

Where today the slogans of a better world spring from his lips, tomorrow there may be nothing but the taste of ashes.

So, precisely at a time when the civil rights movement has achieved its most stirring victories, the revolution of rising expectations demands that we turn now to confront the work which remains.

It is one thing to cry "freedom now" on a picket line. But it is another to achieve true freedom in the squalid world of the ghetto—where generations of exploitation have produced problems which no man can overcome in a day, week, or year —where we see and feel the devastating impact of that tragic equation which has too often decreed that poor shall beget poor and ignorance shall beget misery.

It is one thing to demand the federal government to meet its growing responsibilities in civil rights. But it is another to generate in our states and localities the commitment and urgency required to produce significant improvement in the lives of people.

And it is one thing to overcome flagrant examples of racial prejudice—segregated hotels, buses and parks. But it is another to eliminate the more subtle and sophisticated techniques which effectively restrict true freedom of choice in jobs, education and housing.

Now we must combine an acute sense of urgency with a heightened understanding of the complexity of the remaining civil rights problems. We must balance dedication to action with commitment to achievement.

We must understand there are no easy answers, no instant solutions, to problems generations in the making.

But there are certain problems demanding priority attention as we strive to translate legal promises of equality and freedom into reality.

First, the federal government accepts the job of meeting its growing responsibilities.

One of those responsibilities is to press for legislation to fulfill the promise of the Constitution. You know what this Administration is doing on Capitol Hill to discharge that responsibility—and we need your support urgently if the Civil Rights Act of 1966 is to become law.

There are other responsibilities as well. And one of these is to see that programs financed by all of the people—black and white—shall not be operated to benefit only part of the people.

Last Friday a new day of security and well-being dawned for the senior citizens of this country—the long-awaited program of medicare went into effect.

But another revolution took place simultaneously—a revolution in medical facilities available to Negro Americans and other minorities.

Acting with a clear mandate from Congress, the federal government directed that hospitals could only participate in the medicare program if they provided non-segregated facilities and medical service to persons of all ages.

More than 92 per cent of our hospitals met these standards on July 1—and many of these hospitals were previously segregated. I predict the large majority of those not in compliance will be in the near future.

One fact is certain: the funds for medicare and other federally-assisted facilities are collected without regard to race, color or creed—the benefits, therefore, must and will be available on the same basis.

Secondly, there exists an urgent need for new initiatives and responsibility in civil rights matters by our states and local governments.

The battle against slumism and poverty must be waged

primarily in our local communities—with assistance from the states and federal government.

The struggle to provide quality education for all the children of America must go forward in our localities—again with assistance from the states and federal government.

The job of achieving meaningful choice for all persons in the sale and rental of housing must be accomplished in our cities.

The federal government is fully prepared to play a major role in this process. But the impact of this federal assistance is magnified a thousand-fold if a community is fully committed to the goal of decent, non-segregated housing for all its citizens— if a community is developing creative, bold new approaches to meet the housing crises of urban and rural America.

The vital task of building a system of justice which treats all men alike— black and white, rich and poor—must be carried out in our cities and towns.

"Equal justice under law" is more than a slogan etched over the entrance of the Supreme Court. It is the foundation of our entire democratic system of government.

The Supreme Court has reiterated the need to inform all arrested persons of their right to counsel—of their right not to testify against themselves—and of their right to prompt arraignment before a magistrate.

These decisions—reaffirming some of our fundamental notions of justice in a free society—should be applauded by every American—and implemented by every community.

For in the final analysis, the responsibility for securing equality before the law is a shared responsibility. The judicial, as the legislative and executive branches, has thus posed a challenge to all Americans.

How do we replace the old argument over states' rights with the more meaningful development of states' responsibilities . . . and the responsibilities of communities, and organizations, and individuals?

There is difficult, unglamorous, back-breaking, heartbreaking, day-to-day work ahead in every ghetto . . . every election district . . . and every school district—for only there can our lofty goals and promises be redeemed.

We know the NAACP has been doing this work in countless cities and towns across America. Yes, long ago you made the decision to stay in your communities and do the work that had to be done.

We salute you for this decision.

Yes, I applaud those who left their everyday pursuits to be part of the new birth of freedom taking place in the South.

But I also applaud and honor those who will remain in those towns after the fever pitch of the moment has passed. Theirs is the long and arduous task of converting apathy to conviction—of translating ardor into achievement.

We should strive to do these things because they are proper and just . . . because we have the moral obligation to match our promises with performances and to reward faith with fulfillment.

But we should also do them because this nation will know little tranquility and peace until all Americans have an opportunity to share in her well-being.

We must understand that now the question is not whether all men shall have a full measure of freedom and justice, but how it shall be provided.

Thirdly, we must enlist new allies in our struggle against discrimination and deprivation—from business, labor, religious and community groups.

We know that in recent years impressive strides have been made by both business and labor in rooting out blatant forms of job discrimination based on race or color.

The next phase of the battle will be less dramatic, and it will attract a smaller number of those interested in the simple issues and the easy victories. Yet this next phase—one of the nuts and bolts of the expansion of employment opportunities—is vital.

Outmoded training programs, biased testing and recruitment procedures, apprenticeship requirements and promotion patterns can deny equal employment opportunity as effectively as the old fashioned "white only" classified ads.

We must take vigorous affirmative action through skillfully

designed training programs to help compensate persons who have been denied all opportunity to prepare themselves for today's job market.

We must give special attention to working out equitable procedures so that arrest records, juvenile offenses, and lack of a high school diploma are not permanent barriers to employment where a person has otherwise established his trustworthiness and ability.

Federal departments and agencies are now sponsoring a number of innovative programs so that equal employment opportunity will exist in fact, as well as in law. Private industry must be more willing to experiment as we seek workable solutions to these knotty problems.

The time has come to broaden the base of the civil rights movement . . . to reach out into the community and enlist vital new sources of energy and strength.

Here the NAACP has an especially important role to play. You have traditionally sought close cooperation among churches, labor unions, business groups, and service clubs. We must now reach out even further with the message: "Brother, we need you for freedom."

This appeal cuts to the core of those questions of philosophy and of strategy which currently engage the civil rights movement.

It seems to me fundamental that we cannot embrace the dogma of the oppressors—the notion that somehow a person's skin color determines his worthiness or unworthiness.

Yes, racism is racism—and there is no room in America for racism of any color.

And we must reject calls for racism, whether they come from a throat that is white or one that is black.

Legitimate pride in the achievements and contributions of one's forebears is, of course, another matter. One of the great tragedies of America has been that so few persons—white or black—appreciate the remarkable contributions of Negroes to this nation's history.

How many of us, for example, know that 26 of the 44 settlers who established this city of Los Angeles in 1781 were Negroes?

But pride in Negro history and achievement should establish a basis upon which to build a new climate of mutual respect among all elements of society—not false doctrines of racial superiority. We must strive to create a society in which the aims of the National Association for the Advancement of Colored People and the civil rights movement can be achieved. And, always remember, we seek *advancement . . .* not *apartheid.*

Negroes have been a part of America since Jamestown. They suffered—and survived—the cruel yoke of slavery. They have experienced hardship and discrimination of a severity and duration that no group of Americans has known. And the basis for this brutality has been segregation and exclusion—on terms imposed by the white majority.

Today this system is being torn down through the concerted efforts of both whites and Negroes. We must strive to perfect one citizenship, one destiny for all Americans.

Integration must be recognized as an essential *means* to the *ends* we are seeking—the ends of freedom, justice and equal opportunity for all Americans.

And if there are areas in this country where meaningful integration is not a realistic prospect—as there are, in both the South and the North—then the true remedy lies in creating these conditions as quickly as possible.

As President Johnson said in his historic address at Howard University, "In far too many ways American Negroes have been another nation: deprived of freedom, crippled by hatred, the doors of opportunity closed to hope."

Who, in similar circumstances, might not feel within him the responsive echo to the cries of power and hostile pride?

Who, in similar circumstances, might not finally lose faith and patience with statements of good intention which were seldom translated into action?

Our response to these cries of outrage and despair must be hard, visible evidence—evidence that a man can see and feel and measure in his city . . . his job . . . his home . . . his children . . . his own sense of dignity and self-respect.

Today, after far too long, we are beginning to see that evidence. The road to freedom has been obscured far too many years by hatred and habit, by anger and apathy. But it now lies clearly in view.

We march down that road not in separate columns to the sound of martial music heralding the approach of clashing armies.

We march, instead, together—to the sound of a song echoed by free people everywhere, of all colors, of all races, in every land:

> Stony the road we trod . . .
> Bitter the chastening rod . . .
> Facing the rising sun of our new day begun . . .
> Let us, together, hand-in-hand, march on till victory is
>   won . . .

## CHAPTER FIVE

## *Hubert Humphrey Faces the Black Power Issue*

*Robert L. Scott and Wayne Brockriede*

When Vice President Hubert H. Humphrey spoke to the 1,500 delegates of the NAACP convention in Los Angeles, July 6, 1966, he took a position on the major current issue confronting civil rights groups. Although the issue had not been drawn formally, it was nonetheless divisive. That issue was Black Power.

At about the time Humphrey spoke, Stokely Carmichael said that he had heard the term used in one way and another since he was a child.[1] The phrase did not become a public symbolic issue, however, until it was introduced, presumably by Carmichael, during the Mississippi March which followed the shooting of James Meredith. By June 26, when the march climaxed in Jackson, Miss., Black Power was echoing throughout the country.[2]

SOURCE: This essay was first published in *Speaker and Gavel*, 4, 1 (November, 1966), 11–17. Reprinted by permission of the publisher, Delta Sigma Rho–Tau Kappa Alpha.

[1] Associated Press release from Atlanta, Ga., of an interview with Stokely Carmichael, *Minneapolis Star*, July 7, 1966, p. 1. Carmichael used the Black Power phrase and the Black Panther slogan extensively during SNCC's voter registration drive in Lowndes County, Ala., during the past few years; see Andrew Kopkind, "The Lair of the Black Panther," *New Republic*, Aug. 13, 1966, pp. 10–13. Another interesting use of the phrase prior to the Mississippi March is as the title of a series of articles dealing with Negro politicians during Southern Reconstruction days, 1867–1877. See Lerone Bennett, Jr., "Black Power," *Ebony*, November, 1965, pp. 28–38; December, 1965, pp. 51–60; January, 1966, pp. 116–122; February, 1966, pp. 127–138; April, 1966, pp. 121–131; July, 1966, pp. 58–66; October, 1966, pp. 152–161; December, 1966, pp. 146–158; and January, 1967, pp. 114–122.

[2] See, for example, *Christian Science Monitor*, Midwest Ed., July 11, 1966, p. 1. A useful exposition of the development of the phrase, as well as a perceptive analysis of its issues, is Paul Good, "A White Look at Black Power," *The Nation*, Aug. 8, 1966, pp. 112–117.

By agreeing to speak at the NAACP convention, the Vice
President appeared to signal the approval of the executive
branch of the federal government with the stiffening opposition
of Roy Wilkins and the NAACP and Martin Luther King and
the SCLC toward Floyd McKissick and CORE and Stokely
Carmichael and SNCC, opposition centering on the use of the
Black Power phrase. Indeed, the day before the Humphrey
speech, President Johnson told a news conference, "We are not
interested in black power, and we are not interested in white
power, but we are interested in American democratic power,
with a small 'd.' "[3]
In speaking to the delegates in Los Angeles and, through
reports of the speech, to the nation, Humphrey had three
choices: not to mention or allude to Black Power in any way, to
treat it positively, or to treat it negatively. One might argue
that the first choice was closed: his very being on the program
constituted a position and, further, not to treat the issue would
fail grievously to meet the expectations of his immediate and
larger audiences. Perhaps the President's statements at his press
conference closed the second choice to the Vice President. At
any rate, Humphrey made the third choice.
For the delegates at the NAACP convention and for those
relatively few additional persons who read the complete speech
as a message addressed to those delegates, the speech may well
be judged a masterpiece of identification of the speaker and
what he stands for with the audience and what it stands for.
The strategy of identification is apparent from the outset:
"America is marching on the road to freedom. I am proud to
be back among my friends of the NAACP who have led this
march for 57 years."[4] These words identify both speaker and
audience with a dominant symbol of the civil rights movement,
the march. The speaker recalled the long history of NAACP
involvement in the civil rights march, and many listeners must

[3] *The New York Times*, July 6, 1966, p. 18.
[4] *Congressional Record*, 89th Cong., 2d Sess., July 12, 1966, p. A3609. Mr.
Humphrey's speech was inserted into the *Record* by Senator Warren G.
Magnuson, Washington. All references to the Humphrey speech are to this
printed version, pp. A3607–A3609.

have known the speaker's own dedication to the cause. They may have remembered the 1948 Democratic convention when Humphrey risked his political future in the fight for a strong civil rights plank in the platform. Humphrey may have aided the recollection with his words, "For we have marched . . . even when our band was small and our ranks thin and ragged . . . even when victory seemed a distant and unattainable goal." Throughout the first section of the speech, the "march" motif dominates: "There have been young marchers and old . . . Negro and white . . . rich and poor . . . but always marching with a common spirit—moved by a common hope—and striving for a common objective." The motif suggests gradual progress, hard work, sacrifice, and cooperation; and it identifies the speaker with his NAACP audience.

The second section of the speech develops Humphrey's argument that neither he nor his listeners are, or should be, satisfied with past accomplishments. Civil rights workers and social scientists commonly express the belief that some of the restlessness and frustration in Negro ghettos stems from the male Negro's feeling that he is cut off from a positive, masculine role in his family and his community, cut off in some instances by a lack of education, cut off in others by a lack of opportunity to use what he has. Humphrey seemed to recognize this problem in a significant passage:

> A generation ago, it may have been enough for the Negro to ask for the right to enter a restaurant.
> But today the Negro American asks:
> Is my life better? Are my children attending better schools? Do I hold a better job—or any job? Do I have a voice in the life of my city and my neighborhood? Am I a first class citizen—a man among men, in my own eyes and in the eyes of my family?
> Until a man can truthfully answer "yes" to these questions, we should not expect him to consider the battle won or the struggle ended. And neither should we.

The long middle section of the speech is a catalog of past efforts by the federal government to alleviate conditions that irritate and frustrate, as well as a promise for more action in the future.

The short third section fulfills several functions. Humphrey called for a realistic and cooperative struggle to achieve civil rights for all Americans. He encouraged those of like mind to persevere. The primary function, however, is to support the NAACP leadership on its position on the Black Power issue. One day before the Humphrey speech, Roy Wilkins had taken a vigorous stand on the issue in his keynote address to the delegates:

> No matter how endlessly they try to explain it, the term "black power" means antiwhite power. . . . It has to mean "going it alone." It has to mean separatism.
>
> Now, separatism, whether on the rarefied debate level of "black power" or on the wishful level of a Secessionist Freedom City in Watts, offers a disadvantaged minority little except a chance to shrivel and die. . . .
>
> We of the NAACP will have none of this. We have fought it too long. It is the ranging of race against race on the irrelevant basis of skin color.[5]

The Vice President endorsed Wilkins with a parallel statement on the issue:

> It seems to me fundamental that we cannot embrace the dogma of the oppressor—the notion that somehow a person's skin color determines his worthiness or unworthiness.
>
> Yes, racism is racism—and there is no room in America for racism of any color.
>
> And we must reject calls for racism, whether they come from a throat that is white or one that is black. . . .
>
> We must strive to create a society in which the aims of the National Association for the Advancement of Colored People and the civil rights movement can be achieved. And, always remember, we seek *advancement* . . . not *apartheid*.

[5] See *The New York Times*, July 6, 1966, p. 14, for excerpts from Roy Wilkins' keynote address.

This passage placed Humphrey personally, and by implication the Johnson administration, behind the NAACP and SCLC in their struggle over the Black Power issue with SNCC and CORE. Humphrey had agreed with the majority of delegates who formed his immediate listening audience.[6] Three days after the speech, the convention ended after having passed a resolution described as virtually seeking "to establish the NAACP as the paramount organization that could decide which of the other groups are in the interest of Negroes and of the country, and which are not."[7]

Viewed as an attempt to identify personally and substantively with the NAACP delegates, Humphrey's speech was probably highly successful. Humphrey had joined himself with the goals, values, and positions of the NAACP and its leader, Roy Wilkins.

But the critic has a "second speech occasion" to evaluate when he considers Humphrey's address on July 6. The speaker is Hubert Humphrey as he is revealed through the press and the broadcasting media. The audience is the national audience, especially those persons and groups which have a strong interest in the civil rights movement. The speech consists of excerpts which reporters conveyed to the national audience. With only a few exceptions, press and broadcasting reports limited the "speech" to all or parts of Humphrey's allusion to the Black Power issue in the passage quoted above.[8]

The probable occurrence of the second occasion is predictable.

---

[6] Not all members of the NAACP oppose Black Power. One exception, for example, is the Rev. James Jones, a Negro member of the Los Angeles School Board. In a speech to the NAACP convention, after Wilkins' but before Humphrey's speech, Jones said: "An organization such as the NAACP should not be scared into a position of defense by the power structure with regard to the question of black power [cheers]. The NAACP must accept the challenge of defining black power and making it honorable and a factual part of the total power spectrum in America." Quoted in Nicholas von Hoffman, "Black Power Called Racism by Humphrey," *Washington Post*, July 7, 1966, p. A7.

[7] *Minneapolis Sunday Tribune*, July 10, 1966, p. 4A.

[8] Our treatment of Humphrey's address as two speeches raises an interesting issue in the criticism of contemporary public address. To what extent does the reporter function merely as a channel of communication and to what extent may he be regarded as a more active rhetorical agent, as a part of the source component in a communicative event?

Journalists would find newsworthy what a Vice President might say to a leading civil rights organization about an explosive controversy. Also predictable is the journalists' selection of the passage which relates to the Black Power issue in strikingly figurative language.

Humphrey's "second" speech, addressed through the press to the national audience, may be judged a failure. The rhetorical circumstances, in our judgment, made possible a great speech at a critical moment, but Mr. Humphrey's analysis of the "second" occasion gave him at best a mediocre speech.

The moment was critical because of the nature of Negro need and the nature of the Black Power symbolic issue. Legislative gains had not been transformed into substantial political or economic improvement for Negroes. Discontent was deep, especially in riot-torn and riot-threatened ghettos, and the feeling of powerlessness and frustration to effect significant change led to a sense of desperation. The legislative approach shared by Wilkins and King with the white liberals had become suspect.

Into this sense of need Stokely Carmichael and SNCC had introduced the ambiguous phrase Black Power, and Floyd Mc-Kissick and CORE had endorsed it in Baltimore.[9] The phrase implied *Black* Power, but left open whether the leadership was to be exclusively Negro or whether cooperation with white liberal forces was to be tolerated or sought. It further implied Black *Power*, but left open the specific goals and methods. The phrase threatened, but not clearly, not unequivocally. The black panther's message, "Move on over or we'll move on over you," may be seen as a counterpart to the white rooster and "white supremacy." But the range of power-seeking methods and the degree to which Black Power advocates might move from non-violence through violent self-defense to the initiation of violent acts was yet to be determined.

Though ambiguous (and perhaps, in part, because ambiguous), the phrase developed a fascinating appeal for many Negroes. It spoke to their condition in a way that "freedom now" and nonviolent "we shall overcome" no longer did. Many

[9] See *U.S. News and World Report*, July 18, 1966, p. 31.

Negroes agreed with Floyd McKissick's description of non-violence as a "dying philosophy" that no longer can "be sold to the black people."[10] Black Power developed a kind of rhetorical magical power, and the events of the Mississippi March and the CORE convention revealed many Negroes ready to follow its banner. Where the banner would lead was still negotiable, and the very ambiguity of Black Power implied an attitude mobility inviting to rhetoricians.

How well did Hubert H. Humphrey meet this challenge in his address to the national audience? The first section of the speech to the NAACP delegates failed in its address to the national audience by default. The national audience never heard the "march" motif by means of which Humphrey had so adroitly identified with his physically present audience. Perhaps the journalists viewed this part of the discourse as too ordinary and too predictable to merit reporting.

The second section, again, failed by default. Again, journalists did not report to the national audience Mr. Humphrey's catalog of positive federal achievements, nor did they cite his promises for future action. Humphrey here claimed, "The next phase of the battle will be less dramatic, and it will attract a smaller number of those interested in the simple issues and the easy victories. Yet this next phase—one of the nuts and bolts of employment opportunities—is vital." But Mr. Humphrey did not specify the methods. He only made repeated abstractions of the sort quoted above. To those who are impatient, such promises seem excuses. In short, journalists perhaps properly regarded this portion of the speech as not worth reporting. The Vice President did little to advance the thinking on what gains should be expected through a continuation of the march toward freedom without an exercise of Black Power.

The third section, which journalists channeled to the national audience, failed by employing a negative divisive strategy. In a few well-turned sentences, Mr. Humphrey said "me, too," to Mr. Wilkins' prior rejection of Black Power, and placed the administration behind the NAACP. By implication, the essence

---

[10] *Ibid.*, p. 32.

of the Humphrey message was that Black Power adherents are racists, an accusation certain to alienate such people[11] and tending to force a decision from those who were wondering what attitude to adopt toward the ambiguous phrase, a decision as likely to go toward Black Power as away from it. Not only would a divisive strategy encourage a further splitting of the civil rights movement into two factions, but it would leave the militant faction in full possession of the symbol and in full control of determining its meaning.

"Yet we still think that there tends to be a panicky overreaction to the slogan 'black power,' " a *Christian Science Monitor* editorial said two days after Humphrey's speech.[12] Perhaps the editorial writer could have used the Vice President's speech as a basis for restructuring the response to the term had Humphrey chosen to have spoken differently.

Instead of a strategy of division, saying in effect, "There's the line, cross it at your peril," the Vice President's strategy could have been toward unification. Mr. Humphrey was in a unique position to help heal a breach which two days after the speech Martin Luther King said threatened to split the civil rights movement permanently.[13] Furthermore, he had the opportunity to take the first step toward de-fusing the explosive Black Power phrase.

Did the Vice President really have a good opportunity to unify the movement and to de-fuse the phrase? "No matter how endlessly they try to explain it, the term 'black power' means antiwhite power," Wilkins had said in his keynote address. But that "they" are "endlessly" explaining it indicates that the meaning of the concept is in the process of being worked out. "It is necessary for Negroes to have power," Martin Luther King said in Chicago the day Humphrey spoke in Los Angeles, "We've got to have political power. I don't use the phrase 'black power' because it gives the wrong impression. . . . We do

---

[11] *The New York Times*, July 8, 1966, p. 16, reports that CORE's Floyd McKissick was "visibly angry when asked to comment on remarks made by Mr. Humphrey."

[12] Midwest Ed., July 9, 1966, p. 14.

[13] See *The New York Times*, July 9, 1966, p. 1.

not want to substitute one tyranny for another."[14] Could Mr. Humphrey have helped make Black Power mean political and economic power for Negroes? Certainly the administration stands for increasing Negroes' political and economic power in certain specified ways. Could he have suggested ways in which Negroes might participate more vigorously in achieving certain other specified goals so that power could be used *by* the blacks as well as *for* them?[15] Could he have encouraged civil rights leaders to use the term in less menacing ways?

The person most closely identified with the phrase, Stokely Carmichael, has indicated that the term is open to a pacific interpretation. In his interview with the press the day after Humphrey spoke, he responded to the question, "Roy Wilkins . . . has said no matter how you say it, it means antiwhite. What's your view?" by replying, "Well, I've never used that word and I don't see why the rallying cry of black power would mean that."[16] Mr. Carmichael compared the impulse behind Black Power with the banding together of workers in labor unions to make their demands felt. Here is an analogy that a man like Hubert Humphrey should have been able to see and to exploit.[17]

For the Vice President to have identified himself with a pacific interpretation of Black Power would have recognized the need of Negroes for power exercised in their behalf and also their need to do some of the exercising. It could have aided tendencies toward cooperation and unification of civil rights groups. The strategy is perhaps not an obvious one, nor is it one easily made effective. Given the rhetorical climate in which Mr. Humphrey worked, however, such a choice could have made possible a truly great speech. The choice he made allowed

14 *Minneapolis Star*, July 7, 1966, p. 2A.

15 Martin Luther King recognized this aspect of Black Power: "[If it is] . . . an appeal to racial pride, an appeal to the Negro not to be ashamed of being black, and the transfer of the powerlessness of the Negro into positive, constructive power . . . then I agree with it." Quoted in *Christian Science Monitor*, July 11, 1966, p. 4.

16 *Minneapolis Star*, July 7, 1966, p. 1A.

17 James Jones also suggests the value of defining Black Power (see fn. 7). Had the statement been made by someone as visible as Humphrey, it might have packed a greater rhetorical wallop.

him to identify skillfully with the NAACP and Roy Wilkins. Even assuming the wisdom of rejecting Black Power, however, such a choice allowed the Vice President only to echo Roy Wilkins' keynote address. Given his office and his ability, this much is too little to expect from Hubert Humphrey.

**CHAPTER SIX**

## *Stokely Carmichael Explains Black Power to a Black Audience in Detroit*

Late in July, 1966, Stokely Carmichael, who the month before had made Black Power the issue of an often bitter debate when he introduced the cry into the Meredith March in Mississippi, visited Detroit. He spoke at a number of rallies with candidates for local political offices. On the evening of July 30, he spoke before an audience of Negroes in Cobo Auditorium.

The speech was broadcast by radio station WKNR on August 7. The speech is transcribed here from a tape recording of that broadcast. Unfortunately the speech was edited for the regular half-hour time slot of "Project Detroit." We have not been able to obtain a complete version of the speech. We believe that we have identified accurately the spots from which material has been cut and have indicated those spots with ellipses (. . .).

It was tempting to try to indicate Mr. Carmichael's pronunciation of a number of words with variant spellings, but we decided that to do so would be more detrimental than helpful to understanding and appreciating his speech. Like most speakers delivering an extemporaneous speech before a live audience, he tends to slight many sounds and often omits a simple word in places that standard form would seem to call for. Whereas in listening to a speaker such omissions seem quite natural, they tend to look strange in print.

Any transcription of this sort must be highly arbitrary. We have chosen to write "going to" rather than "gonna" on the grounds that even a fully phonetic rendering would not do justice to Mr. Carmichael and probably would be highly distracting to most readers. On the other hand, we have not inserted the verb "are" when the speaker omits it as he sometimes does before a participle. We did in one place write "ba-a-a-d nigger," since to do otherwise would spoil the joke the speaker and his audience obviously enjoyed sharing.

The matter of punctuating the transcription of any extemporaneous

SOURCE: This speech is printed by permission of SNCC, Atlanta, Ga., and Stokely Carmichael.

speech is likely to be especially troublesome. Commas, colons, periods, and paragraphs are the artifacts of writing, not speaking, even though they may indicate roughly patterns of pauses. What we have done here is only a fair approximation of the pace and phrasing of the speaker. Mr. Carmichael's speech tends to flow quickly from thought to thought, piling phrase on phrase. The high frequency of the conjunction "and" indicates this tendency. To make the punctuation appear conventional enough to keep from distracting readers unduly, we probably have cut up the speech too much.

For the most part, the repetitions which seem needless in print are reflections of the response of the live audience. In listening to Mr. Carmichael's speech, we get the impression of a quick, witty man, alive to the idiom of his audience and inclined to give full feeling to his thought through the sound of his words and their patterns.

I'm going to try to speak the truth. That's very hard to do in this country, you know. A country which was founded on racism and lies. It's very hard to speak the truth. But we're going to try to do that tonight.

Now, these guys—those guys over there. They're called the press. I got up one morning and read a story. They were talking about a cat named Stokely Carmichael. I say he must be a ba-a-a-d nigger [laughter]. For he's raising a whole lot of sand. I had to get up and look in the mirror and make sure it was me [laughter]. Because all I said is that I'm just a poor old black boy, and I think it's time black people stop begging and take what belongs to them [shouts and applause]. And takes what belongs to them [continued applause].

And I said that because I learned that from America. They take what belongs to them. And what don't belong to them, if they can't get it, they destroy it [applause]. So I am not even trying to destroy what don't belong to us. I'm just saying, we going to take it come hell or high water. We going to take what belongs to us. Because it's been taken away from us [applause]. . . .

The reason we're here tonight is we want to talk to black people. We want to talk to black people because the Student Nonviolent Coordinating Committee was founded to help free black people. And when we start talking to black people, everybody gets upset; I wonder why [applause].

I'm going to talk tonight about integration. About what it means. About who it's for. About who it benefits, and what it does to black people. I want to talk about integration tonight. They tell us, and see behind me stands ministers of the Bible, and they will bear me out, that Jesus Christ said, and He's the only man who said, "Only through me shall ye enter into the kingdom of heaven." But what white people say to us with integration is that only through me shall you have better things, that's what they say when they talk about integration [applause].

Yes sir. We're black, and we're poor; and every time we talk about poverty they tell us to join hands with them, that's going to be the answer to our problem. Half the time they don't realize that they are our problem. They are our problem [applause].

They don't even know what integration means. It is the meeting of cultures. Now if they really want to integrate, tell them to move out of Westchester and move into our communities. Tell them to move into Watts; tell them to move into South Side Chicago, if they want to integrate. Tell them to send their lily-white children from the suburbs into our crowded school where they stole money from, send them there. And they're not willing to do that [applause].

We are going to move to better our schools by ourselves. Yes, Lyndon Baines Johnson, we going to go it alone, because that's what we've been doing for lo these four hundred years inside your country. Don't you be ashamed to tell them we going to go it alone. We going to go it alone inside here but outside, brothers, is a whole lot of us waiting to join hands. We may be a minority inside this country, but outside in this world, he's a minority. He'd better learn to realize that [applause]. He'd better learn to realize that [continued applause].

I'm a little bit surprised that Lyndon Baines Johnson, the racist president of this country, can stand up and draw color lines and say ninety per cent against ten per cent—he said it, he drew the color lines. And all the good white folk in the country didn't say to him, "Hunh-uh Lyndon, it's not based on color." They all said, "Well, what you going to do? You only ten per cent." Yeah, we ten percent, brother, but we strewed strategically all over your country, and we've got black brothers in Vietnam [shouts and applause]. We have black brothers in your army, and they may not have woken up yet, but, baby, if you mess with us inside in this country, you going to have a war in Vietnam [applause]. You going to have a war in Vietnam [continued applause].

Let it be known that we don't need threats. This is 1966. It's time out for beautiful words. It's time out for euphemistic statements. And it's time out for singing "We Shall Overcome." It's time to get some Black Power [applause]. It's time to get some Black Power [continued applause].

Now they take our kids out of our community, and they pick the best. You got to be the best to get next to them. You got to be the best to get next to them; they pick the best. The five or six out of every school and send them to their school, and they call that integration. And they tell us that that's the way we going to solve our problem. They leave the rest of our children to stay in the filthy ghettos that they took the money from, and the rest of us get up and say, "Yeah, they working on solving the problem!" Baby, they ain't doing nothing but absorbing the best that we have. It's time that we bring them back into our community [applause].

You need to tell Lyndon Baines Johnson, and all them white folk, that we don't have to move into white schools to get a better education. We don't have to move into white suburbs to get a better house. All they need to do is stop exploiting and oppressing our communities, and we going to take care of our communities. That's what you've got to tell them. You've got to tell them that when a lot of black people get together it doesn't mean that the slum area's going to develop. It's only because we don't own and control our communities that they are the way they are [shouts and applause]. You've got to tell them that [continued applause].

You've got to tell them that if we've got the money, the same amount of money that they put in their suburban schools, that we put in our schools, that we would produce black people who are just as capable of taking care of business, as they're producing white people. They've been stealing our money [applause] that's where the problem exists; we've got to tell them.

Sounds a bit absurd; I'm disturbed by a lot of black people going around saying, "Oh, man, anything all black, it ain't no good." I want to talk to that man. When I was in college, and I went to a black college—they were trying to be white, that was their only problem [applause]. They became so white that the president is now for the war in Vietnam; he's made it in this society, he's integrated fully. Let him stay there [applause].

There's a thing called a syllogism. And it says like, if you're born in Detroit, you're beautiful; that's the major premise. The minor premise is—I am born in Detroit. Therefore, I am beautiful. Anything all black is bad—major premise. Minor premise —I am all black. Therefore [pause], yeah, yeah [laughter and applause] yeah. You're all out there, and the man telling you that anything all black is bad, and you talking about yourself, and you don't even know it. You ain't never heard no white people say that anything all white is bad. You ain't never heard them say it. They only starting to get upset now because we're going for some power. Before they didn't never criticize the fact that their government was all white and was nothing but power, that's white power [applause]. They didn't say nothing about that [continued applause].

Now you've got to be crystal clear on how you think and where you move. You've got to explain to people. I didn't go to Mississippi to fight anybody to sit next to them. I was fighting to get them off my back. That's what my fight is. That's what my fight is. I don't fight anybody to sit next to him. I don't want to sit next to them. I just want them to get the barriers out of my way. Because I don't want to sit next to Jim Clark, Eastland, Johnson, Humphrey, or none of the others, I just want them to get off my back [shouts and applause]. Get off my back [continued applause].

I'm very concerned, because you see we have a lot of Negro leaders, and I want to make it clear that I'm no leader. I represent the Student Nonviolent Coordinating Committee. That's the sole source of my power, and that's Black Power. I'm no Negro leader, but I think that we have to speak out about the war in Vietnam. We've got to talk to black people about the war in Vietnam. This country has reduced us, black people, to such a state that the only way our black youths can have a decent life is to become a hired killer in the army [applause]. Don't you know that? I'm going to speak the truth tonight. That when a man can get up to say, "Well the best chance any Negro can have of course is to go into the Armed Forces and, therefore, that's why there's so many of them." Do you mean to tell me for me to have a decent life I've got to become a hired killer and fight it out in Vietnam? Baby, it's time we stayed here and fight it out here [shouts and applause]. That's where we going to fight it out; that's where we going to stay [continued applause].

You take a man, and you send him to Vietnam, a black man; and he's fighting to give free elections to North Vietnam, that's what they tell us, it's a lie, but that's what they tell us. And that same black man who's fighting to give free elections to a North Vietnamese can't even have free elections in Alabama, Louisiana, Mississippi, Georgia, Tennessee, Arkansas, Louisiana [sic], and Washington D.C. [applause]. That man is nothing but a black mercenary. A mercenary is a hired killer, and Western civilization knows a lot about mercenaries—they invented them. They used them in the Congo not too long ago. They using them now in Vietnam. You send a black man to Vietnam to fight for rights, and he doesn't have any rights in his homeland, he's a black mercenary. You send a black man to Vietnam, and he gets shot and killed fighting for his country; and you bring him home, and they won't bury him in his land—he's a black mercenary [applause]. He's a black mercenary [continued applause]. And if we going to be black mercenaries, then they ought to pay us twenty-five thousand dollars a year and let us come home every weekend [laughter and applause]. Since they not going to do that, we going to have to develop in our communities enough internal strength to tell everyone in this country that we're not going to your damn war period [shouts and applause]. We've got to do that [continued applause]. . . .

We have to start looking to Africa, brothers and sisters. We've got to tell our African brothers that we talking about Black Power for them, too. Black Power so they can get up and take arms and shoot the hell out of the white folk in South Africa. That what we've got to tell them [shouts and applause]. That what we've got to tell them [continued applause]. Because we going to move to tell them that once they control South Africa, then Standard Oil's going to be reduced to our position, they going to be begging, too. We've got to tell them to get rid of Chase Manhattan Bank in South Africa. We've got to tell them it's time they told the missionaries to take their bibles and go back to Europe and preach the white man's burden there where it belongs [applause]. That's what we've got to tell them [continued applause]. That's what we've got to tell them.

Rudyard Kipling made a mistake. The white man's burden should have been preached in England. He should have left us alone. They came with the Bibles, and we had the land; they left with the land, and we got the Bibles [applause]. Yes, we've got to tell the brothers in South Africa that all that gold and diamonds and oil is theirs, and they've got to get some Black Power and control it. That's what they've got to do. And we've got to tell the black brothers in Africa that we stand one hundred per cent behind Mr. Nkrumah; he's our man, he's our man [applause]. We've got to tell them [continued applause]. We've got to tell them.

But you've got to open your eyes and understand what's going on in this world. And we've got to tell our African brothers that we were hep to the World Court. We knew the United States was giving a racist country like Australia two votes so they could make believe they were voting on their side; we going tell them we hep. We know what's happening. Brother, it's 1966 and we been here for years and our eyes are open wide. And we seeing you clear through, and you're nothing but a racist country, and you've built and live upon sweat and blood of our black skins and we're standing up today, we're standing up [applause]. We're standing up [continued applause].

Now I'm no Negro leader, so I don't ever apologize for any black person. And don't you ever apologize for any black person who throws a Molotov cocktail [shouts and applause]. Don't you ever apologize [continued applause]. And don't you ever call those things riots, because they are rebellions, that's what they are [applause]. That's what they are [continued applause]. And the truth of the matter is that they're not organized because if they were we'd get a hell of a lot more besides sprinklers on hydrants [shouts and applause].

And we've got to stand tall in this time and tell the man just where it's at. And you've got to let your organizations not act as a buffer zone between you and the man. But tell the man the way you telling it, and if they not doing that, move them out the way, move them out the way [applause].

Now we've got to talk about this thing called the serious coalition. You know what that's all about? That says that black folks and their white liberal friends can get together and overcome. We have to examine our white liberal friends. And I'm going to call names this time around. We've got to examine our white liberal friends who come to Mississippi and march with us, and can afford to march because our mothers, who are their maids, are taking care of their house and their children; we got to examine them [applause]. Yeah; I'm going to speak the truth tonight. I'm going to tell you what a white liberal is. You talking about a white college kid joining hands with a black man in the ghetto, that college kid is fighting for the right to wear a beard and smoke pot, and we fighting for our lives [cheers and applause]. We fighting for our lives [continued applause].

That missionary comes to the ghetto one summer, and the next summer he's in Europe, and he's our ally. That missionary has a black mammy, and he stole our black mammy from us. Because while she was home taking care of them, she couldn't take care of us. That's not our ally [applause]. Now I met some of those white liberals on the march, and I asked one man, I said, look here brother. I said, you make what, about twenty-five thousand dollars a year? He mumbled. I said, well dig. Look here. Here are four black Mississippians. They make three dollars a day picking cotton. See they have to march; you can afford to march. I say, here's what we do. Take your twenty-five thousand dollars a year divide it up evenly. Let all five of you make five thousand dollars a year. He was for everybody working hard by the sweat of their brow [laughter and shouts]. That's a white liberal, ladies and gentlemen. That's a white liberal. You can't form a coalition with people who are economically secure. College students are economically secure; they've already got their wealth; we fighting to get ours. And for us to get it is going to mean tearing down their system, and they are not willing to work for their own destruction. Get that into your own minds now [applause]. Get that into your own minds now [continued applause].

Now we want to talk about the great white father of Detroit [shouts and laughter]. I'm talking about master-captain-boss-man Walter Reuther. Yes, sir. I want to talk about that white man, that great white father [applause]. Now that's our friend. Let me explain something to you just politically about our friend. Mr. Reuther is a man who speaks for organized labor. Most of our youths are unemployed. Are you hep to that? Understand that very clearly. Organized labor in this country are fighting to keep what they have and leave the people unemployed, and we're joining the unemployment ranks everyday, and you're talking about he's our friend. You ain't got no sense politically. You ain't got no sense politically. And that man is talking from a base of Black Power, more Black Power than black politicians are talking from a base of Black Power. He goes and talks about Black Power. He says I have so many black people in my organization. They can deliver so many votes. He using Black Power to tell you not to talk about it; you sitting there saying uh-huh, umhumm [applause].

You talking about joining hands with a white liberal, the great white father, Walter Reuther; and that man is for the war in Vietnam. Where is your political sense? We can't afford to be for the war in Vietnam, but our friend is for twenty-two per cent of the people being shot in Vietnam, us; he's our friend [applause]. He's our friend. Baby, I know who my enemies are, but God will have to deliver us from our friends. I'm afraid, gentlemen, that you're going to have to pray every night for help from our friends; we going to need it, we sure need it. Now that's what we've got to talk about.

We have unemployment ranks growing every day. Reuther's not concerned about unemployed people; that's us, we have to be concerned about our youth for a change, and stop being concerned about the image of a filthy country that's racist. We have to be concerned about us and not the image of this country [shouts and applause]. That's what we have to be concerned about [continued applause].

See we have to begin to define success. See we don't have any longer to prove to them that we're all the things that they say that we're not. Ralph Bunche has done that and now he's just like them. Carl T. Rowan has done that and we can't even tell him any more. George Schyler is up there, and I've got to look hard and find out whether he is or he is not. It's time for us to say to our black brothers that success is going to mean coming back into your community and using your skills to help develop your people [applause].

It's time that we say to our doctors—yes, that we don't want to hear this garbage about you charging twenty-five dollars for us, because that's what they do uptown, if you went up there they'd do the same thing. Let that man know that he gets his money from us; and he ought to be lucky if we pay him fifty cents when he sees us because we ain't got no money. We got to define success for our black doctors. We've got to tell them that they ought not to charge us any money because we can't afford to pay it. Talking about charging ten dollars for a visit because that's what the white man does uptown. And he's making money off of us. Next time he does that tell him to go uptown and charge the white man ten dollars [laughter and applause].

Yes sir, we've got to get our black lawyers. We've got to bring them in here. We got to tell them that we understand they moving now to give us some protection after we got beat up by some white power—in our communities. And we've got to say to those lawyers, we want you to be aggressive. We want you to get back the districts that they just gerrymandered and took away from us. Get them back now. We want you to be aggressive. Move to disband the white power forces, the gestapo troops that beat us up every Friday night and Saturday night. Move to displace them; we want you to be aggressive. Work for us for a change, gentlemen [shouts and applause].

Gentlemen, we want to talk about nonviolence. We want to say that nonviolence has to begin to be taught in our neighborhoods. We have to teach ourselves to love and respect each other. Because the psychology of that man has worked on us, and we're trying to destroy each other every Friday and Saturday night. That's where we're going to preach nonviolence and nowhere else [shouts and applause]. That's where we're going to preach nonviolence [continued applause]. That's where we're going to preach nonviolence [continued applause].

Yes, brothers and sisters, we're going to move to talk to our young brothers who are gang members. We're going to bring them together, and we going to have some real energy in this country. We're going to tell them that they ought not to be shooting and killing each other. Because you understand, you got to understand the psychology of Western civilization; it is a master race. It is a master race. They think they're the masters of the world. They think that they're God and nobody has a right to hate them, that's what they think [continued applause]. That's what they think.

It's all right, it's all right for you to hate your brother and cut him up on Friday night and Saturday night; but don't even hate them if they're exploiting you, that's no good. They think they're masters of the world; they think they God. And we've got to tell them, "Baby, you ain't God, we've just let you play for a couple of hundred years [shouts and applause]."

And now it's time out for play. We've got to bring them to their knees. We've got to build a power base that will be our protection. That if they touch one black man in California while he's taking his wife to the hospital, if they touch one black man in Mississippi while he's walking down the highway, if they touch a group of black people riding their horses on their day off in Detroit, that we will move to disrupt this whole damned country [applause]. We've got to tell them [continued applause].

And we had better understand that we going to have to go it alone. And don't be ashamed of that brothers and sisters, because we're very Christian. They taught us about David and Goliath [shouts and applause]. . . .

When I talk about Black Power, it is presumptuous for any white man to talk about it, because I'm talking to black people [applause]. And I've got news for our liberal friend Bobby Kennedy. I got news for that white man. When he talks about his Irish Catholic power that made him to the position where he is that he now uses black votes in New York City to run for the presidency in 1972, he ought to not say a word about Black Power. Now the Kennedys built a system of purely Irish Catholic power with Irish Nationalism interwoven into it. Did you know that? And that's how come they run, rule, own Boston lock stock and barrel including all the black people inside it. That's Irish power. And that man going to get up and tell you-all; well he shouldn't talk about Black Power. He ran and won in New York City on Black Power; his brother became president because Black Power made him president [shouts and applause]. Black Power made his brother president [continued applause]. And he's got the white nerve to talk about Black Power [continued applause]. . . .

## CHAPTER SEVEN

## *Stokely Carmichael Explains Black Power to a White Audience in Whitewater, Wisconsin*

From the fall of 1966 to the spring of 1967, Stokely Carmichael toured the United States speaking repeatedly, often to white audiences. Many of these appearances were on college campuses; in fact, he usually spoke three or four times a week to such audiences. His speech on the campus of Wisconsin State University in Whitewater, February 6, 1967, is probably typical. After a brief extemporaneous introduction, he read an essay to his audience, in this case "Toward Black Liberation" (*Massachusetts Review*, Autumn, 1966, pp. 639–651; Carmichael refers to the periodical in his introduction as the "Massachusetts Quarterly"). Although in reading he did become confused at one point and have to begin a sentence again, saying, "Sorry. I got ahead. The trouble with reading anything, you got to stick with it. If you try to run your own thoughts, you get ahead," Carmichael delivered his written thought smoothly and easily.

We have transcribed the introduction from a tape recording of the speech. Since Carmichael's deviations from his text are few, we have chosen to use the essay as he wrote it. We have indicated a few deviations in making a transition from our transcription to the essay.

Thank you very much. It's a cold honor to be here tonight. I was just telling Mr. Hoover [the chairman of the meeting] that I am sure that the professors must have mandated you to come because if I came to this university, only Ben Bella

source: The essay "Toward Black Liberation," *Massachusetts Review*, Autumn, 1966, pp. 639–651, which constitutes the bulk of this speech is copyrighted by the Student Nonviolent Coordinating Committee. Reprinted by permission of SNCC, Atlanta, Ga., and Stokely Carmichael.

would be able to get me out of the dormitory on a night like this [laughter], and he has to come back from wherever he is at now.

I have a problem in deciding which article to read [holding the articles]. One I wrote in early September which appeared in the *New York Review of Books* which I condensed. The tighter, and the next one is one that appeared in the fall issue of the "Massachusetts Quarterly." And I still haven't decided yet. I think I'll read the one in the "Massachusetts Quarterly" because it's much tighter.

Oh, I notice on the leaflets that they were passing around there was a thing that said that I was now facing a charge of inciting to riot. And I just wanted to clarify that a little. In Atlanta they have a man by the name of Ivan Allen who is mayor and he's called a progressive. And I agree, he is a progressive racist [laughter]. Well there was a rebellion in Atlanta in early September, and I happened to show up at the place, and Mr. Allen needed a scapegoat so he arrested me two nights later for inciting to riot. And put a ten thousand dollar bail on my head. When I was in jail, then the black Atlanta community began to riot with signs saying to get me out of jail. They then came and asked me to get out. And I told them, no, I liked it much better inside [laughter]. They dropped the charge of inciting to riot two days later and dropped the ten thousand dollar bail. And then to save face, charged me with something called rioting. Well, of course, I'm not satisfied with that. Now we did want a chance to fight Mayor Allen. So we brought an injunction against him which was entitled Stokely Carmichael versus Ivan Allen, *et al.* And we won that injunction—the newspapers didn't tell you that—which means that every one of the ninety people who were arrested must be freed on the charge of rioting. The Student Nonviolent Coordinating Committee has never ever been implicated in that riot.

And I thought I'd just clarify that for you. Newspapers don't do that. They're advertisers at heart. We live in a growing society of advertisement.

I wanted to introduce to you one of our organizational secretaries who accompanied me here if he didn't get lost in the cold. There he is. Stanley Wise. Stanley [applause].

[At this point, there was some adjusting of the microphone and inquiries by the chairman about whether or not people sitting in the back of the auditorium could hear. Finally someone shouted, "We can hear you, not him." This remark underscores the fact that Stokely Carmichael is generally quite soft-spoken, TV news film clips to the contrary notwithstanding, and gave him the opportunity to make the following remarks].

Well, I'll tell you why you can't hear me [laughter]. When I was small, I used to come home, and I'd say to my mother, "Ma, ma, I'm home." Now she'd say, "Shhh, Negroes are too loud" [laughter]. So since I didn't want to be Negro, since then I've tried to become soft [Carmichael laughed and the crowd joined].

The article deals with a theoretical outline; the brothers got that [referring to his companions; then, general laughter]. You let us have one in joke, won't you?

The article deals with a theoretical background for the need of Black Power. It attacks politically the concept of integration, and then goes on to show the shortcomings of the exponents of coalition theory. The main exponent notably being Mr. Bayard Rustin. I want to make it crystal clear that I do not attack anybody in terms of an *ad hominem* attack. But I attack their political philosophy.

[At this point, Carmichael reads his essay. He consistently changes the word "Negro" which he used in his article to "black." In addition, he underscores his feeling that the press has been quite unfair to him. He also expands his negative remarks toward the Johnson-Humphrey administration. The failure to seat the 1964 Mississippi Freedom delegates is clearly highly significant for Carmichael. "We call him handkerchief head Humphrey, that is like a 'yes man,' like a frog; you know, Johnson says 'jump' and Humphrey says, 'How high boss man?' " Carmichael also repeats a sentence from *The New York Times* advertisement he reads early in the essay,

"We are faced now with a situation where powerless conscience meets conscience-less power," saying that that is "axiomatic to race relations in America."]

One of the most pointed illustrations of the need for Black Power, as a positive and redemptive force in a society degenerating into a form of totalitarianism, is to be made by examining the history of distortion that the concept has received in national media of publicity. In this "debate," as in everything else that affects our lives, Negroes are dependent on, and at the discretion of, forces and institutions within the white society which have little interest in representing us honestly. Our experience with the national press has been that where they have managed to escape a meretricious special interest in "Git Whitey" sensationalism and race-war mongering, individual reporters and commentators have been conditioned by the enveloping racism of the society to the point where they are incapable even of objective observation and reporting of racial *incidents*, much less the analysis of *ideas*. But this limitation of vision and perceptions is an inevitable consequence of the dictatorship of definition, interpretation and consciousness, along with the censorship of history that the society has inflicted upon the Negro—and itself.

Our concern for Black Power addresses itself directly to this problem, the necessity to reclaim our history and our identity from the cultural terrorism and depredation of self-justifying white guilt.

To do this we shall have to struggle for the right to create our own terms through which to define ourselves and our relationship to the society, and to have these terms recognized. This is the first necessity of a free people, and the first right that any oppressor must suspend. The white fathers of American racism knew this—instinctively it seems—as is indicated by the continuous record of the distortion and omission in their dealings with the red and black men. In the same way that southern apologists for the "Jim Crow" society have so obscured, muddied and misrepresented the record of the reconstruction period, until it is almost impossible to tell what really happened, their contemporary counterparts are busy doing the same thing with the recent history of the civil rights movement.

In 1964, for example, the National Democratic Party, led by L. B. Johnson and Hubert H. Humphrey, cynically undermined the efforts of Mississippi's black population to achieve some degree of political representation. Yet, whenever the events of that convention are recalled by the press, one sees only that version fabricated by the press agents of the Democratic Party. A year later the House of Representatives in an even more vulgar display of political racism made a mockery of the political rights of Mississippi's Negroes when it failed to unseat the Mississippi Delegation to the House which had been elected through a process which methodically and systematically excluded over 450,000 voting-age Negroes, almost one half of the total electorate of the state. Whenever this event is mentioned in print it is in terms which leaves one with the rather curious impression that somehow the oppressed Negro people of Mississippi are at fault for confronting the Congress with a situation in which they had no alternative but to endorse Mississippi's racist political practices.

I mention these two examples because, having been directly involved in them, I can see very clearly the discrepancies between what happened, and the versions that are finding their way into general acceptance as a kind of popular mythology. Thus the victimization of the Negro takes place in two phases—first it occurs in fact and deed, then, and this is equally sinister, in the official recording of those facts.

The Black Power program and concept which is being articulated by SNCC, CORE, and a host of community organizations in the ghettos of the North and South has not escaped that process. The white press has been busy articulating their own analyses, their own interpretations, and criticisms of their own creations. For example, while the press had given wide and sensational dissemination to attacks made by figures in the civil rights movement—foremost among which are Roy Wilkins of the NAACP and Whitney Young of the Urban League—and to the hysterical ranting about black racism made by the political chameleon that now serves as Vice-President, it has generally failed to give accounts of the reasonable and productive dialogue which is taking place in the Negro community, and in certain important areas in the white religious and intellectual community. A national committee of influential Negro Churchmen affiliated with the National Council of Churches, despite their obvious respectability and responsibility, had to resort to a paid advertisement to articulate their position, while anyone shouting the hysterical yappings of "Black Racism" got ample space. Thus the American people have gotten at best a superficial and misleading account of the very terms and tenor of this debate. I wish to quote briefly from the statement by the national committee of Churchmen which I suspect that the majority of Americans will not have seen. This statement appeared in the *New York Times* of July 31, 1966.

> *We an informal group of Negro churchmen in America are deeply disturbed about the crisis brought upon our country by historic distortions of important human realities in the controversy about "black power." What we see shining through the variety of rhetoric is not anything new but the same old problem of power and race which has faced our beloved country since 1619.*
> *. . . The conscience of black men is corrupted because, having no power to implement the demands of conscience, the concern for justice is transmuted into a distorted form of love, which in the absence of justice becomes chaotic self-surrender. Powerlessness breeds a race of beggars. We are faced now with a situation where powerless conscience meets conscience-less power, threatening the very foundations of our nation.*
> *. . .* We deplore the overt violence of riots, but we feel it is more important to focus on the real sources of these eruptions. These sources may be abetted inside the ghetto, but their basic causes lie in the silent and covert violence which white middleclass America inflicts upon the victims of the inner city.

. . . In short: the failure of American leaders to use American power to create equal opportunity *in life* as well as *in law*, this is the real problem and not the anguished cry for black power.

. . . Without the capacity to *participate with power, i.e.,* to have some organized political and economic strength to really influence people with whom one interacts—integration is not meaningful.

. . . America has asked its Negro citizens to fight for opportunity as *individuals*, whereas at certain points in our history what we have needed most has been opportunity for the *whole group*, not just for selected and approved Negroes.

. . . We must not apologize for the existence of this form of group power, for we have been oppressed as a group, not as individuals. We will not find our way out of that oppression until both we and America accept the need for Negro Americans, as well as for Jews, Italians, Poles, and white Anglosaxon Protestants, among others, to have and to wield group power.

Traditionally, for each new ethnic group, the route to social and political integration into America's pluralistic society, has been through the organization of their own institutions with which to represent their communal needs within the larger society. This is simply stating what the advocates of Black Power are saying. The strident outcry, *particularly* from the liberal community, that has been evoked by this proposal can only be understood by examining the historic relationship between Negro and white power in this country.

Negroes are defined by two forces, their blackness and their powerlessness. There have been traditionally two communities in America. The white community, which controlled and defined the forms that all institutions within the society would take, and the Negro community which has been excluded from participation in the power decisions that shaped the society, and has traditionally been dependent upon, and subservient to the white community.

This has not been accidental. The history of every institution of this society indicates that a major concern in the ordering and structuring of the society has been the maintaining of the Negro community in its condition of dependence and oppression. This has not been on the level of individual acts of discrimination between individual whites against individual Negroes, but as total acts by the white community against the Negro community. This fact cannot be too strongly emphasized —that racist assumptions of white superiority have been so deeply ingrained in the structure of the society that it infuses its entire functioning, and is so much a part of the national subconscious that it is taken for granted and is frequently not even recognized.

Let me give an example of the difference between individual racism and institutionalized racism, and the society's response to both. When unidentified white terrorists bomb a Negro church and kill five children, that is an act of individual racism, widely deplored by most segments of the society. But when in that same city, Birmingham, Alabama, not five but five hundred Negro babies die each year because of a lack of proper food, shelter and medical facilities, and thousands more are destroyed and maimed physically, emotionally and intellectually because of conditions of poverty and deprivation in the ghetto, that is a function of institutionalized racism. But the society either pretends it doesn't know of this situation, or is incapable of doing anything meaningful about it. And this resistance to doing anything meaningful about conditions in that ghetto comes from the fact that the ghetto is itself a product of a combination of forces and special interests in the white community, and the groups that have access to the resources and power to change that situation benefit, politically and economically, from the existence of that ghetto.

It is more than a figure of speech to say that the Negro community in America is the victim of white imperialism and colonial exploitation. This is in practical economic and political terms true. There are over twenty million black people comprising 10 percent of this nation. They for the most part live in well-defined areas of the country—in the shanty-towns and rural black belt areas of the South, and increasingly in the slums of northern and western industrial cities. If one goes into any Negro community, whether it be in Jackson, Miss., Cambridge, Md. or Harlem, N.Y., one will find that the same combination of political, economic, and social forces are at work. The people in the Negro community do not control the resources of that community, its political decisions, its law enforcement, its housing standards; and even the physical ownership of the land, houses, and stores *lie outside that community.*

It is white power that makes the laws, and it is violent white power in the form of armed white cops that enforces those laws with guns and nightsticks. The vast majority of Negroes in this country live in these captive communities and must endure these conditions of oppression because, and only because, *they are black and powerless.* I do not suppose that at any point the men who control the power and resources of this country ever sat down and designed these black enclaves, and formally articulated the terms of their colonial and dependent status, as was done, for example, by the Apartheid government of South Africa. Yet, one can not distinguish between one ghetto and another. As one moves from city to city it is as though some malignant racist planning-unit had done precisely this—designed each one from the same master blueprint. And indeed, if the ghetto had been formally and deliberately planned, instead of growing spontaneously and inevitably from the racist functioning of the various institutions that combine to make the society, it would be somehow less frightening. The situation would be less frightening because, if these ghettos were the result of design and conspiracy, one could understand their similarity as being artificial and consciously imposed, rather than the result of identical patterns of white racism which repeat themselves in cities as distant as Boston and Birmingham. Without bothering to list the historic factors which contribute to this pattern— economic exploitation, political impotence, discrimination in employment and education—one can see that to correct this pattern will require far-reaching changes in the basic power-relationships and the ingrained social patterns within the society. The question is, of course, what kinds of changes are necessary, and how is it possible to bring them about?

In recent years the answer to these questions which has been given by most articulate groups of Negroes and their white allies, the "liberals" of all stripes, has been in terms of something called "integration." According to the advocates of integration, social justice will be accomplished by "integrating the Negro into the mainstream institutions of the society from which he has been traditionally excluded." It is very significant that each time I have heard this formulation it has been in terms of "the Negro," the individual Negro, rather than in terms of the community.

This concept of integration had to be based on the assumption that there was nothing of value in the Negro community and that little of value could be created among Negroes, so the thing to do was to siphon off the "acceptable" Negroes into the surrounding middle-class white community. Thus the goal of the movement for integration was simply to loosen up the restrictions barring the entry of Negroes into the white community. Goals around which the struggle took place, such as public accommodation, open housing, job opportunity on the executive level (which is easier to deal with than the problem of semi-skilled and blue collar jobs which involve more far-reaching economic adjustments), are quite simply middle-class goals, articulated by a tiny group of Negroes who had middle-class aspirations. It is true that the student demonstrations in the South during the early sixties, out of which SNCC came, had a similar orientation. But while it is hardly a concern of a black sharecropper, dishwasher, or welfare recipient whether a certain fifteen-dollar-a-day motel offers accommodations to Negroes, the overt symbols of white superiority and the imposed limitations on the Negro community had to be destroyed. Now, black people must look beyond these goals, to the issue of collective power.

Such a limited class orientation was reflected not only in the program and goals of the civil rights movement, but in its tactics and organization. It is very significant that the two oldest and most "respectable" civil rights organizations have constitutions which *specifically* prohibit partisan political activity. CORE once did, but changed that clause when it changed its orientation toward Black Power. But this is perfectly understandable in terms of the strategy and goals of the older organizations. The civil rights movement saw its role as a kind of liaison between the powerful white community and the dependent Negro one. The dependent status of the black community apparently was unimportant since—if the movement were successful—it was going to blend into the white community anyway. We made no pretense of organizing and developing institutions of community power in the Negro community, but appealed to the conscience of white institutions of power. The posture of the civil rights movement was that of the dependent, the suppliant. The theory was that without attempting to create any organized base of political strength itself, the civil rights movement could, by forming coalitions with various "liberal" pressure organizations in the white community—liberal reform clubs, labor unions, church groups, progressive civic groups—and at times one or other of the major political parties—influence national legislation and national social patterns.

I think we all have seen the limitations of this approach. We have repeatedly seen that political alliances based on appeals to conscience and decency are chancy things, simply because institutions and political organizations have no consciences outside their own special interests. The political and social rights of Negroes have been and always will be negotiable and expendable the moment they conflict with the interests of our "allies." If we do not learn from history, we are doomed to repeat it, and that is precisely the lesson of the Reconstruction. Black people were allowed to register, vote and participate in politics because it was to the advantage of powerful white allies to promote this. But this was the result of white decision, and it was ended by other white men's decision before any political base powerful enough to challenge that decision could be established in the southern Negro community. (Thus at this point in the struggle Negroes have no assurance—save a kind of idiot optimism and faith in a society whose history is one of racism—that if it were to become necessary, even the painfully limited gains thrown to the civil rights movement by the Congress will not be revoked as soon as a shift in political sentiments should occur.)

The major limitation of this approach was that it tended to maintain the traditional dependence of Negroes, and of the movement. We depended upon the good-will and support of various groups within the white community whose interests were not always compatible with ours. To the extent that we depended on the financial support of other groups, we were vulnerable to their influence and domination.

Also the program that evolved out of this coalition was really limited and inadequate in the long term and one which affected only a small select group of Negroes. Its goal was to make the white community accessible to "qualified" Negroes and presumably each year a few more Negroes armed with their passport—a couple of university degrees—would escape into middle-class America and adopt the attitudes and life styles of that group; and one day the Harlems and the Watts would stand empty, a tribute to the success of integration. This is simply neither realistic nor particularly desirable. You can integrate communities, but you assimilate individuals. Even if such a program were possible its result would be, not to develop the black community as a functional and honorable segment of the total society, with its own cultural identity, life patterns, and institutions, but to abolish it—the final solution to the Negro problem. Marx said that the working class is the first class in history that ever wanted to abolish itself. If one listens to some of our "moderate" Negro leaders it appears that the American Negro is the first race that ever wished to abolish itself. The fact is that what must be abolished is not the black community, but the dependent colonial status that has been inflicted upon it. The racial and cultural personality of the black community must be preserved and the community must win its freedom while preserving its cultural integrity. This is the essential difference between integration as it is currently practiced and the concept of Black Power.

What has the movement for integration accomplished to
date? The Negro graduating from M.I.T. with a doctorate
will have better job opportunities available to him than to
Lynda Bird Johnson. But the rate of unemployment in the
Negro community is steadily increasing, while that in the
white community decreases. More educated Negroes hold executive jobs in major corporations and federal agencies than
ever before, but the gap between white income and Negro
income has almost doubled in the last twenty years. More
suburban housing is available to Negroes, but housing conditions in the ghetto are steadily declining. While the infant
mortality rate of New York City is at its lowest rate ever in
the city's history, the infant mortality rate of Harlem is steadily
climbing. There has been an organized national resistance
to the Supreme Court's order to integrate the schools, and
the federal government has not acted to enforce that order.
Less than 15 percent of black children in the South attend
integrated schools; and Negro schools, which the vast majority
of black children still attend, are increasingly decrepit, over-
crowded, under-staffed, inadequately equipped and funded.

This explains why the rate of school dropouts is increasing
among Negro teenagers, who then express their bitterness, hope-
lessness, and alienation by the only means they have—rebellion.
As long as people in the ghettos of our large cities feel that
they are victims of the misuse of white power without any
way to have their needs represented—and these are frequently
simple needs: to get the welfare inspectors to stop kicking down
your doors in the middle of the night, the cops from beating
your children, the landlord to exterminate the vermin in your
home, the city to collect your garbage—we will continue to have
riots. These are not the products of Black Power, but of the
absence of any organization capable of giving the community
the power, the Black Power, to deal with its problems.

SNCC proposes that it is now time for the black freedom
movement to stop pandering to the fears and anxieties of the
white middle class in the attempt to earn its "good-will," and
to return to the ghetto to organize these communities to control themselves. This organization must be attempted in

northern and southern urban areas as well as in the rural black belt counties of the South. The chief antagonist to this organization is, in the South, the overtly racist Democratic Party, and in the North the equally corrupt big city machines.

The standard argument presented against independent political organization is "But you are only 10 percent." I cannot see the relevance of this observation, since no one is talking about taking over the country, but taking control over our own communities.

The fact is that the Negro population, 10 percent or not, is very strategically placed because—ironically—of segregation. What is also true is that Negroes have never been able to utilize the full voting potential of our numbers. Where we could vote, the case has always been that the white political machine stacks and gerrymanders the political subdivisions in Negro neighborhoods so the true voting strength is never reflected in political strength. Would anyone looking at the distribution of political power in Manhattan, ever think that Negroes represented 60 percent of the population there?

Just as often the effective political organization in Negro communities is absorbed by tokenism and patronage—the time honored practice of "giving" certain offices to selected Negroes. The machine thus creates a "little machine," which is subordinate and responsive to it, in the Negro community. These Negro political "leaders" are really vote deliverers, more responsible to the white machine and the white power structure, than to the community they allegedly represent. Thus the white community is able to substitute patronage control for audacious Black Power in the Negro community. This is precisely what Johnson tried to do even before the Voting Rights Act of 1966 was passed. The National Democrats made it very clear that the measure was intended to register Democrats, not Negroes. The President and top officials of the Democratic Party called in almost one hundred selected Negro "leaders" from the Deep South. Nothing was said about changing the policies of the racist state parties, nothing was said about repudiating such leadership figures as Eastland and Ross Barnett in Mississippi or George Wallace in Alabama.

What was said was simply "Go home and organize your people into the local Democratic Party—*then* we'll see about poverty money and appointments." (Incidentally, for the most part the War on Poverty in the South is controlled by local Democratic ward heelers—and outspoken racists who have used the program to change the form of the Negroes' dependence. People who were afraid to register for fear of being thrown off the farm are now afraid to register for fear of losing their Head-Start jobs.)

We must organize black community power to end these abuses, and to give the Negro community a chance to have its needs expressed. A leadership which is truly "responsible"— not to the white press and power structure, but to the community—must be developed. Such leadership will recognize that its power lies in the unified and collective strength of that community. This will make it difficult for the white leadership group to conduct its dialogue with individuals in terms of patronage and prestige, and will force them to talk to the community's representatives in terms of real power.

The single aspect of the Black Power program that has encountered most criticism is this concept of independent organization. This is presented as third-partyism which has never worked, or a withdrawal into black nationalism and isolationism. If such a program is developed it will not have the effect of isolating the Negro community but the reverse. When the Negro community is able to control local office, and negotiate with other groups from a position of organized strength, the possibility of meaningful political alliances on specific issues will be increased. That is a rule of politics and there is no reason why it should not operate here. The only difference is that we will have the power to define the terms of these alliances.

The next question usually is, "So—can it work, can the ghettos in fact be organized?" The answer is that this organization must be successful, because there are no viable alternatives—not the War on Poverty, which was at its inception limited to dealing with effects rather than causes, and has become simply another source of machine patronage. And

"Integration" is meaningful only to a small chosen class within the community.

The revolution in agricultural technology in the South is displacing the rural Negro community into northern urban areas. Both Washington, D.C. and Newark, N.J. have Negro majorities. One third of Philadelphia's population of two million people is black. "Inner city" in most major urban areas is already predominantly Negro, and with the white rush to suburbia, Negroes will in the next three decades control the heart of our great cities. These areas can become either concentration camps with a bitter and volatile population whose only power is the power to destroy, or organized and powerful communities able to make constructive contributions to the total society. Without the power to control their lives and their communities, without effective political institutions through which to relate to the total society, these communities will exist in a constant state of insurrection. This is a choice that the country will have to make.

CHAPTER EIGHT

## Stokely Carmichael: Two Speeches on Black Power

*Wayne Brockriede and Robert L. Scott*

When during the Meredith march in Mississippi in June, 1966, Stokely Carmichael thrust himself and the phrase Black Power into public controversy, students of rhetoric might have asked themselves two questions. In the inevitable interchange which would filter through the mass media to the public at large, what meaning would emerge as dominant for a phrase obviously ambiguous enough to generate many interpretations? What principal image would people develop of Stokely Carmichael, a man capable of evoking many attitudes toward himself?

On July 6, 1966, the Vice-President of the United States spoke to the convention of the NAACP in Los Angeles. In an analysis of that speech we argued that the term Black Power permitted a pacific interpretation and that Hubert Humphrey was in an excellent position to take the lead in defusing the explosive content of the term while expediting its constructive potential.[1] The Vice-President chose, rather, to follow the lead of Roy Wilkins in emphasizing the belligerently divisive thrust of the term by suggesting adroitly that it was simply "black racism."

The month following Humphrey's speech, a member of the federal administration did say that "it is hard to know yet what the term means to the average Negro. . . . But if it

SOURCE: This essay was first published in the *Central States Speech Journal*, **19**, 1 (Spring, 1968), 3–13. Reprinted by permission of the publishers, the Central States Speech Association.

[1] Robert Scott and Wayne Brockriede, "Hubert Humphrey Faces the Black Power Issue," *Speaker and Gavel*, **4**, 1 (November, 1966), pp. 11–17.

means assertive action by the various splinter groups to achieve full political, economic, and social equality, then good will come of it."[2] But Assistant United States Attorney General for civil right John M. Doar did not hold the position to command widespread national attention nor was a speech before the convention of the National Bar Association, "a largely negro group," as the *Detroit News* put it, an important occasion compared with the NAACP Convention.

The immediate response saw few probing to locate a basis for making the term constructive; indicative is Martin Luther King's statement on July 9, 1966, that Black Power threatened to split the civil rights movement permanently.[3] The next month, however, Rev. Andrew J. Young, the executive director of King's Southern Christian Leadership Conference, conceded that SNCC's, position on Black Power "isn't too far from ours except in style and semantics."[4]

Just as the phrase Black Power permits several interpretations, the man Stokely Carmichael generates several images. Relatively few, however, now see Carmichael as Robert Lewis Shayon did when he wrote, after hearing him interviewed on WBAI-FM, that he discerned "a plausible human being firm in conviction and purpose, but quietly rational."[5]

Within a few months of the advent of Carmichael and Black Power and continuing to this moment, one meaning and one image thoroughly has engulfed the public mind and has dominated the attitudes of most white liberals: Black Power is violent racism in reverse, and Stokely Carmichael is a monster. Late last year, an Associated Press dispatch pictured Carmichael taking his place on "Bertrand Russell's tribunal deliberating alleged U.S. war crimes in Vietnam" and being "wel-

[2] *Detroit News*, Aug. 4, 1966, p. 8D.

[3] *The New York Times*, July 9, 1966, p. 1.

[4] Quoted in Paul Good, "A White Look at Black Power," *The Nation*, Aug. 8, 1966, p. 115; see also Frank Millspaugh, "Black Power," *Commonweal*, Aug. 5, 1966, pp. 500–503.

[5] "The Real Stokely Carmichael," *Saturday Review*, July 9, 1966, p. 42; see also Robert Penn Warren, "Two for SNCC," *Commentary*, April, 1965, pp. 38–48, and T. George Harris, "Negroes Have Found a Jolting New Answer," *Look*, June 27, 1967, pp. 30–31.

comed by the first 'witness' on the stand . . . [that day] Pham
Ngoc Thach, North Vietnam's health minister."[6] Carmichael's
odyssey from August to December, 1967, occasioned anti-
American propaganda from Havana to Hanoi and across North
Africa. His actions are taken, of course, as verification of
the quick negative response to Carmichael and to Black Power.
Yet this response seems lamentably to miss an opportunity to
respond to a plausible challenge, not a demonic threat, and to
reconcile views which were far from irreconcilable. Eric Hoffer's
"a bishopric conferred on Luther at the right moment might
have cooled his ardor for a Reformation"[7] is far too strong to
be applied wistfully to Carmichael. But he and his slogan de-
served to be taken seriously.

The purpose of this essay is to examine the rhetoric of Stokely
Carmichael and to try to answer two questions: (1) What were
the rhetorical strategies? (2) What accounted for the predominantly negative response to the man and his message? We shall
focus on two speeches which seem to illustrate well the characteristic strategies. One was made to a predominantly Negro
audience in Detroit on July 30, 1966.[8] The other was delivered
to a predominantly white audience in Whitewater, Wisconsin,
February 6, 1967. Actually, the substance of the latter speech is
an essay published in the Autumn, 1966, issue of the *Massachusetts Review*.[9] The two speeches, therefore, are in a sense
nearly simultaneous efforts to express Carmichael's views on
Black Power to markedly different audiences.

[6] *Minneapolis Star*, Nov. 29, 1967, p. 17A.

[7] *The True Believer*, New York, Harper & Row, Publishers, 1951, p. 132.

[8] The speech was delivered in Cobo Auditorium (*Detroit News*, July 31,
1966, p. 8A). A tape recording was broadcast by radio station WKNR on
Aug. 7, 1966. The speech was edited somewhat to fit the time allotted the
half-hour program "Project Detroit." Quotations from the speech come
from our transcription of the broadcast.

[9] After a brief extemporaneous introduction, Carmichael announced to his
Whitewater audience that he would read either an article he had written
for *The New York Review of Books* (see Sept. 22, 1966, pp. 5–8) or an article
from the "Massachusetts Quarterly." He chose the latter saying that it was
"tighter" and read, with some extemporaneous comments, an article from
the *Massachusetts Review* [Stokely Carmichael, "Toward Black Liberation,"
7, 4 (Autumn 1966), pp. 639–651]. Quotations will be from the article
except for extemporaneous remarks which are transcribed from a complete
tape recording of the speech and question period.

Before examining the strategies, we should make explicit our assumption that Stokely Carmichael is decidedly a rhetorician. The two speeches we are analyzing are outstanding examples of audience adaptation. Carmichael's fundamental thought is highly consistent in both speeches—he makes many of the same points and strikes essentially the same posture in making them. The two speeches differ distinctly in style and in persuasive appeals, however; in each instance style and appeals are appropriate to the audience addressed. Carmichael seemed to repeat one or the other of these two speeches on other occasions, varying each "with the audience, the area, the news that day, [and] his mood."[10] Carmichael himself seems to recognize, and worry about, his rhetorical tendencies. He reveals his recognition and anxiety in an interview with Robert Penn Warren, conducted more than a year before Carmichael became well-known:

> You've got to think about whether or not you're opportunistic. It bothers me a lot. If I see my name in the paper, I'm not sorry it's there. When you write and say you want to interview me, I'm not sorry, I feel sort of good. That's one of the things you have to be worried about. The trouble is that you get an opportunist, and he becomes a rhetorician, he says things that are going to appease people, he's not going to really look for solutions.[11]

A year later few people would accuse him of a rhetoric of appeasement, but his advocacy of Black Power was very much the actions of a rhetorician.

### I

What were Carmichael's rhetorical decisions?

First, he decided to address himself primarily to a black audience. *Newsweek* reports that Carmichael charged white audiences $1000.00 for "a rather tame exposition of black power" and Negro colleges $500.00 for "the gloves-off treat-

[10] Bernard Weinraub, "The Brilliancy of Black," *Esquire*, January, 1967, p. 132.
[11] Warren, *op. cit.*, pp. 47–48.

ment."[12] More significantly, when speaking to mixed audiences or through the mass media to the general public, he aims his appeals at black people. Bruce Detweiler explained the rationale for this decision:

> In the early days of the movement, when organizations were appealing to whites, SNCC gave the word "Freedom" its magical ring. Now the appeal is to disenfranchised Negroes, and now the cry is "Black Power." For political reasons, and for their own dignity, Negroes must learn to do their own bidding politically and economically.[13]

In following the strategy of aiming primarily at Negroes, Carmichael personified the ideology he was advancing and aimed at identification with his chosen primary audience.

Second, he decided to compress his ideology into the ambiguous slogan Black Power. For Carmichael the slogan seems to carry three major implications: personal pride in being black, responsibility to other blacks, and power as a group to deal with outsiders.

Foremost among the implications of his ideology is his insistence that black people, as a matter of personal pride, must assume the right to define their own identity, their relation to the total society, and the meaning of such important terms as Black Power. He explained the significance of this right to his predominantly white audience at Whitewater:

> Our concern for Black Power addresses itself directly to this problem, the necessity to reclaim our history and our identity from the cultural terrorism and depredation of self-justifying white guilt.
> To do this we shall have to struggle for the right to create our own terms through which to define ourselves and our relationship to the society, and to have these terms recognized. This is the first necessity of a free people, and the first right that any oppressor must suspend.[14]

---

12 "Which Way for the Negro?" *Newsweek*, May 15, 1967, p. 28.
13 "A Time to Be Black," *New Republic*, Sept. 17, 1966, p. 22.
14 Carmichael, *op. cit.*, pp. 639–640.

Carmichael urged that black people must define "what freedom is, what a white liberal is, what black nationalism is, what power is."[15] He insisted that at this point in the struggle only Negroes "can preach to other Negroes in the fight for identity and power."[16] Although responsibility and independence are reflected in these statements, unquestionably one of his major motives is to stress black pride. He underscored this concern in the Detroit speech:

> I'm disturbed by a lot of black people running around saying, "Oh, man, anything all black, it ain't no good." I want to talk to that man. . . . You ain't never heard no white people say anything all white is bad. You ain't never heard them say it.

Carmichael views Black Power as a "black declaration of independence. It is a turn inward, a rallying cry for a people in the sudden labor of self-discovery, self-naming, and self-legitimization."[17]

Black identity and black pride must be mobilized into a group effort to improve the black community. This second implication of Carmichael's ideology is sharply pragmatic. Clearly it has evolved out of his observation of the effects of the black-white coalition to integrate individual Negroes. To the Whitewater audience, he said:

> Also the program that evolved out of this coalition was really limited and inadequate in the long term and one which affected only a small select group of Negroes. Its goal was to make the white community accessible to "qualified" Negroes and presumably each year a few more Negroes armed with their passports—a couple of university degrees—would escape into middle-class America and adopt the attitudes and life styles of that group; and one

[15] Quoted in Lerone Bennett, Jr., "Stokely Carmichael: Architect of Black Power," *Ebony*, September, 1966, p. 28.

[16] Quoted in "Marching Where?" *Reporter*, July 14, 1966, p. 16.

[17] Quoted in Bennett, *loc. cit.*

day the Harlems and the Watts would stand empty, a tribute to the success of integration.[18]

To Carmichael the assumptions behind integration are highly suspect: At best, the Negro abolishes himself; more realistically, a few integrate while conditions in the ghettos grow steadily worse. Carmichael is more concerned with institutionalized racism, the systematic oppression of a whole race, than with individualized racism. His goal is to improve the lot of black people *as a group,* rather than to have a few educated black people absorbed into white society each year. He told his Whitewater audience, "You can integrate communities, but you assimilate individuals."[19]

Carmichael's objection to individualized integration, apart from its slow futility, is that it weakens the black community as a whole. Of the integration of schools and housing, he told his black audience in Detroit:

> Baby, they ain't doing nothing but absorbing the best that we have. It's time that we bring them back into our community [applause]. You need to tell Lyndon Baines Johnson and all them white folk that we don't have to move into white schools to get a better education. We don't have to move into white suburbs to get a better house. All they need to do is stop exploiting and oppressing our communities and we going to take care of our communities.

To realize this brave assertion means keeping the best-educated, most able Negroes working for the community interest. Carmichael concludes:

> We have to begin to define success. . . . It's time for us to say to our black brothers that success is going to mean coming back into your community and using your skills to help develop your people.

18 Carmichael, *op. cit.,* p. 647.
19 *Ibid.*

Carmichael was trying to build a sense of community among black people.

The most difficult ideological question relates to the meaning of "power." The issue is this: Where on the continuum between nonviolent political, economic, social, and cultural influence and violent rebellion does Carmichael's Black Power belong? The only certain conclusion is that no one can be certain. The WKNR announcer who introduced Carmichael's Detroit speech on the "Project Detroit" radio broadcast said:

> Black power has been damned by most; praised by few, if any. . . . Most have interpreted Carmichael's phrase [as] . . . "the greatest setback for the cause of the Negro and civil rights in this century." Others, and they have been few, argue that all Carmichael means is political and economic power—the Negro population uniting.

But the minority version is plausible. Carmichael has often argued that black votes have too often benefited others and that black politicians are apt to be the puppets of white-dominated major parties. In an interview with Gordon Parks, he stressed Black Power as a political and economic bloc which would serve its own purposes first.

> *We* pick the brother and make sure he fulfills *our* needs. Black Power doesn't mean anti-white, violence, separatism or any other racist thing the press says it means. It's saying, "Look, buddy, we're not laying a vote on you unless you lay so many schools, hospitals, playgrounds and jobs on us."[20]

To his Wisconsin audience Carmichael put his interpretation in the mainstream of American ideals: "Traditionally, for each new ethnic group, the route to social and political integration into America's pluralistic society, has been through the organization of their own institutions with which to represent their com-

[20] *Life*, May 19, 1967, p. 82.

munal needs within the larger society."[21] Yet in the same speech the overtones of violence also appear, as in this passage referring to the ghettos:

> These areas can become either concentration camps with a bitter and volatile population whose only power is the power to destroy, or organized and powerful communities able to make constructive contributions to the total society. Without the power to control their lives and their communities, without effective political institutions through which to relate to the total society, these communities will exist in a constant state of insurrection.[22]

The suggestion of violent resistance is even stronger in the Detroit speech:

> I'm no Negro leader, so I don't ever apologize for any black person. And don't you ever apologize for any black person who throws a Molotov cocktail [applause]. Don't you ever apologize [continued applause]. And don't you ever call those things riots, because they are rebellions, that's what they are [applause]. That's what they are [continued applause].[23]

In his speeches before predominantly white audiences, the hints of rebellion and support for violence in self-defense are undeniable in Carmichael's amplification of the meaning of power. Yet even in his speeches before predominantly black audiences, one finds nowhere in his rhetoric an espousal of violence for the sake of violence. The stress throughout is on improving the black community through a call for group pride and support for "*independent* political, social, economic, and

---

21 Carmichael, *op. cit.*, p. 642. For a further discussion of this interpreta-tion, see Millspaugh, *op. cit.*, p. 500.

22 Carmichael, *op. cit.*, p. 651.

23 In the extemporaneous asides and, especially, in the question period of the Whitewater speech, Carmichael's tone is closer to that in the Detroit speech than it is in the article he is reading; but even so, the threatening temper never reaches the pitch of the Detroit speech.

cultural institutions that . . . [Black Power] can control and use as instruments of social change."[24]

In addition to his decision to concentrate his rhetoric on the black audience and to present an ideology appropriate primarily for that audience, Stokely Carmichael seems to have made a third rhetorical decision—the choice to project an image and to utilize a style which would reinforce the ideology by a personal identification with his chosen audience.

The quotations already cited from his Detroit speech reflect his attempt to identify stylistically. A contrast of these with the quotations from his Whitewater speech suggests that Carmichael's attempt to adjust his style to his audience is a conscious choice. He shows his awareness of his urge to identify in answering a question after a speech in the fall of 1966 at an interracial camp at Glen Falls, Vermont: "As a person oppressed because of my blackness, I have common cause with other blacks who are oppressed because of *their* blackness."[25] Bernard Weinraub describes Carmichael's delivery when speaking to black audiences:

> He shakes his head as he begins speaking and his body appears to tremble. His voice, at least in the North, is lilting and Jamaican. His hands move effortlessly. His tone —and the audience loves it—is cool and very hip. . . . No preacher harangue. No screaming. He speaks one tone above a whisper, but a very taut, suppressed whisper.[26]

The desire, obviously, is to be perceived not as a pedestalled "Negro leader," but as a peer.

The answer to our first major question, then, is that Stokely Carmichael formed an ideology for a black audience with whom he identifies stylistically. We turn now to a second question: Why did the selection of these rhetorical strategies result in such an overwhelmingly negative reaction from the public at large and especially from many white liberals who had long supported strenuously the civil rights movement?

[24] Quoted in Bennett, *loc. cit.*
[25] Quoted in Weinraub, *op. cit.*, p. 134.
[26] *Ibid.*, p. 132.

## II

The most important response to this question is that the white audience received a distorted version of the message and the image. In commenting on Vice-President Humphrey's speech to the NAACP Convention, we noted the role of the press in reporting to the "second audience," to the general public, emphasizing that the passage labeling Black Power as "racist" was consistently reported and that nothing else in the speech was.[27] The role of the press in transmitting the rhetoric of Stokely Carmichael, with a vigorous reinforcement from the power structure, was to disambiguate the Black Power message into violent racism and to filter a complex and ambivalent Carmichael into a simple and satanic Stokely.

Carmichael is aware, of course, of the role of the press in his Black Power campaign. In his Whitewater speech, he argued that Negroes have suffered continually from press distortion:

> One of the most pointed illustrations of the need for Black Power, as a positive and redemptive force in a society degenerating into a form of totalitarianism, is to be made by examining the history of distortion that the concept has received in national media of publicity. In this "debate," as in everything else that affects our lives, Negroes are dependent on, and at the discretion of, forces and institutions within the white society which have little interest in representing us honestly.[28]

He makes a similar point with bitter humor in the Detroit speech:

> Now these guys. Those guys over there. They're called the press. I got up one morning and read a story. They were talking about a cat named Stokely Carmichael. I say he must be a bad nigger [laughter]. For he's raising a

[27] Scott and Brockriede, *op. cit.*, p. 14.
[28] Carmichael, *op. cit*, p. 639; see also Carmichael's statement quoted in Millspaugh, *op. cit.*, p. 500, and in Good, *op. cit.*, p. 114.

whole lot of sand! I had to get up and look in the mirror and make sure it was me.

Although most Americans are apt to shrug off such complaints as simply to be expected of those they perceive as radicals, Carmichael's claim that he and Black Power were not represented fairly can be supported. How did the press distort the message and filter the image?

Selective reporting is heavily accountable. Seldom did the mass media report anything designed to develop a constructive interpretation of Black Power. A long story in the *Detroit News*, for example, reported Carmichael's visit and the speech analyzed in this essay, but it contained little more than a count of the audience at the Cobo Auditorium and at various rallies, emphasizing with unmistakable satisfaction that Carmichael was not drawing well in the Negro community.[29] A dozen column inches include no reference to any of the ideas he articulated so challengingly. Furthermore, when Lyndon Johnson, Hubert Humphrey, and Roy Wilkins repudiated Black Power, they got front-page coverage. For the most part, reports of support for the concept were buried in the back pages.

Perhaps even more damaging was the way the broadcasting media sharpened a single, simple, unambiguous caricature of Carmichael. T. George Harris describes the treatment:

> White ears discriminate. The public hears Negroes best when they sound wild . . . or beg for welfare. . . . [When Stokely Carmichael] tries to define his Black Power motto in terms of economic and political development, he finds himself shouting into deaf ears. But when, pacing like a panther, he twists himself into a trance, snarling terror, he makes the evening TV news for millions of very alert people, both races. . . . Carmichael mutters at the invincible stupidity of reporters—but cannot resist performing in their spotlight.[30]

[29] *Detroit News*, July 31, 1966, p. 8A.
[30] Harris, *loc. cit.*

Robert Lewis Shayon lamented the "monster treatment" by two major TV newscasts which gave Carmichael the "air of militancy. . . . That's all there was to the portrait—short, sharp, demagogic." After commenting on a more sympathetic treatment on WBAI-FM, Shayon drew this incisive conclusion:

> Now, you may argue that the civil rights leader, speaking in a white man's studio, was making white man's talk in sweet reasonableness, but that the television cameras saw more truly when he was pep-talking people down South. You may be right. It is also possible that the real Stokely Carmichael embraces both images (which of us talks singly in all roles?). The fact remains that people fortunate enough to [hear the] . . . broadcast have a great deal more evidence before them to account for this man and his meaning to the present struggle for human rights than is available to the viewers who saw only the monster-half of the story on television.[31]

Given the message and the image most people received, could they not be expected to reject them? The interesting question for students of rhetoric is the speculation about what might have been. Had the mass media presented more shades of meaning in Black Power and a fuller portrait of Carmichael, how then would white liberals have responded?

Carmichael's strategies relating to his choice of audiences, of ideology, and of modes of identification might have caused most white liberals to reject Black Power even had they received a more complete version. They might have been antagonized by the stress he put on talking to black listeners. Although he often made this choice on the rational basis of redressing a past imbalance ("Black leaders have been running across town so long worrying about what white people are saying that they don't know what it means to stay at home and worry about what black people are saying"[32]), often he seemed simply, irrationally to deny interest in communicating to white audiences ("We

[31] Shayon, *loc. cit.*
[32] Quoted in Bennett, *loc. cit.*

don't have to explain anything to anybody. . . . Your job is to understand us"[33]). Furthermore, when Carmichael did speak to white audiences, he sometimes wearied in the struggle to communicate to them. When a white girl in the Wisconsin audience asked him to define Black Power after he had dealt with the term explicitly in his speech, he shrugged her off and missed an opportunity to underscore his claim that whites must pay serious attention. At other times he seems to close the possibility of dialogue with white men altogether. For example, he told his Detroit audience, "When I talk about Black Power, it is presumptuous for any white man to talk about it, because I'm talking to black people." He recognized what he was doing and also a possible consequence of the strategy: "Whites get nervous when we don't keep talking about brotherly love. They need reassurance. But we're not about to divert our energies to give it to them."[34]

However, in spite of Carmichael's disclaimers, he did try to communicate with white audiences as well as black. As early as the Meredith march in June, 1966, at the beginning of the public controversy over Black Power, Bruce Detweiler reports that he was particularly impressed with Carmichael's "eagerness to communicate his ideas to the whites who would listen to him."[35] After a militant speech, according to Gene Roberts, "White liberals or newsmen will draw Carmichael aside and ask if 'black power' is really an antiwhite philosophy, and often Mr. Carmichael will say, 'Of course not.' . . . Carmichael is so sincere and convincing during these private explanations that many of his questioners come away believing that they completely missed the point of his public utterances."[36]

Clearly, Carmichael seems to have put different constructions on Black Power for different groups of listeners. But the poten-

[33] Quoted in Gene Roberts, "The Story of Snick: From 'Freedom High' to 'Black Power,' " *The New York Times Magazine*, Sept. 25, 1966, p. 120.
[34] Quoted in Good, *op. cit.*, p. 114; for similar statements by Carmichael concerning the importance of concentrating primarily on black audiences, see Weinraub, *op. cit.*, p. 134. Detweiler, *loc. cit.*; and *Life*, May 19, 1967, p. 82.
[35] Detweiler, *op. cit.*, p. 20.
[36] Roberts, *op. cit.*, p. 128.

tiality for strengthening the pacific interpretation was present for some white listeners to capitalize on. Carmichael was intent on this interpretation when speaking before audiences like that at Whitewater, and in writing for publications like the *Massachusetts Review* and the *New York Review of Books*. He wrote a letter to the *New York Times Magazine* in which he disputed statements in Gene Roberts' article (cited above) concerning SNCC's promotion of Ivanhoe Donaldson and his own arrest in Atlanta.[37] Carmichael wanted to talk to both black and white people. He wanted to challenge white audiences to a new relationship with blacks. On the balance, he was more concerned with the latter than with the former; he may have been at fault in often suggesting a violent specter. Regardless, had the press contributed to the potential dialogue by presenting a fuller view of Carmichael and Black Power, white liberals might have been less threatened and more able to respond constructively to what they were too prone to take as a wholly hostile ideology from a satanic spokesman.

How might they have responded to the three ideological implications of Black Power had they perceived them as challenges rather than threats? White liberals might have recognized, first of all, the need for black people to assume pridefully the leadership in defining the terms and goals of the struggle for black justice and equality. They might have recognized that their own leadership and that of such moderates as Martin Luther King and Roy Wilkins no longer appeared meaningful and effective to many Negroes in the ghettos to whom the gains of civil rights legislation had not gone. A new leadership had emerged, and the old coalition had disintegrated. The civil rights movement, which, in the words of David Danzig, "originated with whites and at its height became a nationwide coalition of whites and blacks, now faces the prospect of becoming an all-black movement."[38] Danzig argues that such a change was inevitable:

> The dilemma is real and cannot be escaped by blaming
> the Negro militants for alienating white supporters by

[37] *The New York Times Magazine*, Oct. 16, 1966, pp. 98–100.
[38] "In Defense of Black Power," *Commentary*, September, 1966, p. 43.

their anti-white rhetoric: even if every Negro in America daily professed his great love for the whites, the coalition would still be breaking up for having fulfilled so much of the civil-rights program which brought it together, and for having no program on which it can agree to deal with the economic plight of the Negro masses.[39]

In part because white liberals did not hear Carmichael's full message and in part because they seemed not to listen carefully to what they did hear, they inferred that Carmichael was saying that black people had no further need for them in any way. A more accurate inference is that black people wanted to control the definition and direction of their own independent movement, but that Black Power does not necessarily imply that whites may not cooperate with that movement in the formation of a new coalition. Perhaps Carmichael might have increased the likelihood of a coalition of equals had he stressed more the constructive challenge implicit in the message. Instead, perhaps because another emphasis was attractive to his primary audience, Carmichael hammered at the failure of the old coalition and his dogged determination to reject it. "We got to examine our white liberal friends," he told his Detroit audience. No doubt many of those who so counted themselves were deeply wounded by the accusations that they were serving their own interests and using Negroes to their own ends. Carmichael was fond of citing the failure of the 1964 Democratic Convention to seat the Mississippi Freedom delegates and of the House of Representatives to "unseat the Mississippi Delegation to the House which had been elected through a process which methodically and systematically excluded over 450,000 voting-age Negroes."[40] White freedom marchers, again, might be inclined to mark both the ingratitude and inaccuracy of Carmichael's charge that they could afford to march because colored maids were taking care of things back home.[41]

No one can doubt that Carmichael failed to solve the dilemma

[39] *Ibid.*, p. 46.
[40] Carmichael, *op. cit.*, p. 640.
[41] Detroit speech.

of facing two audiences. Totally ignoring white listeners would have been a serious error (given the nature of the root problem) and in the end impossible (given the mass media). Perhaps had Carmichael been less extreme in speaking to Negroes he would have been less inclined to alienate nonblacks, but he would have paid dearly in his effort to develop pride in a black movement. Nonetheless, had a more complete picture of the ambiguous, ambivalent Carmichael enabled more listeners to perceive the rhetorical dilemmas he faced and the priority of his intentions, the overall liberal response might have been more constructive.

What about the response to the second ideological implication of Black Power—the need to improve the conditions of the entire group? Again, perhaps Carmichael's emphasis unfortunately may have reinforced the simplified message common to the mass media's treatment—unalterable opposition to integration. He did often attack the consequences of integration; he told his Detroit audience, "I'm going to talk tonight about integration. About what it means. About who it's for. About who it benefits. And what it does to black people. I want to talk about integration tonight" [shouts and applause]. Even as sympathetic an observer as Bayard Rustin concluded that Black Power is "a slogan directed primarily against liberals by those who once counted liberals among their closest friends."[42] Those who had long regarded "integration" as a god-word predictably resented the attack on their concept.

Yet if liberals had listened carefully to Carmichael's position on integration, they might have realized that his opposition was to *individualized* integration which, he argued convincingly, was not an effective antidote to *institutionalized* racism. They might have accepted Carmichael's shift from a goal of integrating "qualified" individuals to the goal of integrating the black community as a whole into a society. This ambitious goal may well have entailed changes in society that many liberals would approve on quite different grounds. Again, of course, the mass media did not channel the subtleties of Carmichael's distinctions, and by the time white liberals had access to the full mes-

---

[42] " 'Black Power' and Coalition Politics," *Commentary,* September, 1966, p. 40.

sage they may have conceived so rigidly Carmichael's position as being anti-integration and anti-white that they could not hear the position as pro-integration of the black *community*.

Finally, had the press channelled Carmichael's full ideology, white liberals might have been challenged to search for new ways of achieving power rather than being threatened to fear riots. They might have seen as compatible with their own values such statements as occurred in the Whitewater speech:

> We must organize black community power to end these abuses, and to give the Negro community a chance to have its needs expressed. A leadership which is truly "responsible"—not to the white press and power structure, but to the community—must be developed. Such leadership will recognize that its power lies in the unified and collective strength of that community. This will make it difficult for the white leadership group to conduct its dialogue with individuals in terms of patronage and prestige, and will force them to talk to the community's representatives in terms of real power.[43]

They might have heard Carmichael claim, as he did several times during the question period at Whitewater, that Negroes are acting in self-defense. They might, at least, have recognized the ambiguity of "power" and sought to develop relatively peaceful meanings for the term rather than to assume, with the press and Establishment spokesmen, that power means violence. They might have recognized, with Bayard Rustin, the tragedy that would follow if "white liberals allowed verbal hostility on the part of Negroes to drive them out of the movement or to curtail their support for civil rights. The issue was injustice before 'black power' became popular, and the issue is still injustice."[44]

Carmichael's ability to identify stylistically with his audience was both an asset and a liability. When speaking to black or mixed audiences, he identified with Negroes. His rhetorical decisions left him no other choice. But the tendency of the mass

[43] Carmichael, *op. cit.*, p. 650.
[44] Rustin, *op. cit.*, p. 39.

media to present predominantly this image to the general public undercut the potential effect of his ability to speak the language of the white audience. He did not, of course, take the position of subservient supplicant—his message and his character precluded that choice; but his style did reflect a man genuinely interested in interacting with white audiences and being not only recognized as an equal but also as a representative of a distinct community. Had more liberal leaders been fully exposed to the sort of speaking Carmichael did at Whitewater, a constructive interpersonal dialogue would have been much more likely.

In this essay we have examined Stokely Carmichael's strategies in choosing an audience, an ideology, and a mode of identification. The general public reacted negatively to his rhetoric; most tragic is that most liberals apparently failed to react differently. At this writing, Carmichael seems to be removed effectively, both physically and figuratively, from any position to be an active voice for change *within* our society. Black Power is virtually a synonym for threatened violence; it has the slenderest possibility of being transformed to a constructive rallying cry.

Since Carmichael's image and his slogan will continue to haunt our hopes and fears in the days ahead, we ought to ask how we can account for the initial failures. The reasons seem to be threefold.

First, the mass media conveyed only part of the man and his message to the mass audience. Students of contemporary rhetoric must re-examine the role of media specialists. The presumption that a journalist functions only to channel passively a rhetorician's message to a mass audience seems altogether unwarranted. Rather, a journalist is himself an active agent who makes rhetorical decisions of his own which may or may not be compatible with those of the rhetorician he reports. Press Power seems to have defeated Black Power in a battle of unequals.

Second, Carmichael himself might have increased his chances of persuading white liberals by making clearer to them how they could become involved in a new coalition dedicated to new goals which were compatible with their own values and motives. Perhaps he reasoned, however, that to go very far in communicating this message might have jeopardized his primary message to his primary audience. Perhaps to carry both rhetorical burdens demanded more ability than Carmichael has. To do both adequately would be truly remarkable.

Third, white liberals must bear a substantial share of responsibility for reacting so quickly and so thoughtlessly to the distorted image and partial message and for having failed to have caught the total thrust of the rhetoric of Stokely Carmichael and Black Power.

## CHAPTER NINE

# Justifying Violence: The Rhetoric of Militant Black Power

*Robert L. Scott*

This is a real revolution. Revolution is always based on land. Revolution is never based on begging somebody for an integrated cup of coffee. Revolutions are never based upon love-your-enemy and pray-for-those-who-spitefully-use-you. And revolutions are never waged singing "We Shall Overcome." Revolutions are based upon bloodshed. Revolutions are never compromising. Revolutions are never based upon any kind of tokenism whatsoever. Revolutions overturn systems. And there is no system on this earth which has proven itself more corrupt, more criminal, than this system that in 1964 still colonizes 22 million African-Americans, still enslaves 22 million Afro-Americans.[1]

These are the words of Malcolm X. But Malcolm X is dead.[2] Since he spoke these words in 1964, 101 major riots have

SOURCE: This essay was first published in the *Central States Speech Journal*, **19**, 2 (Summer, 1968), 96–104. Reprinted by permission of the publishers, the Central States Speech Association. As some readers might surmise from the tone of the oral harangue that still permeates the essay, it is based on a speech—to be more specific, on a paper—Mr. Scott read at the convention of the Central States Speech Association in Chicago, Apr. 6, 1968.

[1] Quoted in George Breitman (ed.), *Malcolm X Speaks*, New York, Grove Press, Inc., 1966, p. 50.

[2] He was assassinated in New York City, Feb. 21, 1965. Some militants are now arguing that his shooting was a CIA plot, as did Matthew Eubanks in a speech in Minneapolis (see *Minneapolis Tribune*, Feb. 25, 1968, p. 12B). Some are arguing that Negroes need black holidays to unite. Although

paralyzed our major cities; 130 people have been killed and 3,623 injured. The total cost is set at 714.8 million dollars.[3] Although these figures do not match the body counts nor the dollar counts from Vietnam, they are enough to make "revolution" seem less a hyperbole than it did in 1964.

Malcolm X is dead, but his words echo in the speeches of Stokely Carmichael, H. Rap Brown, John Hulett, Harry Edwards, Herman B. Ferguson, Fred Brooks, and others. In January 1965, speaking of revolutionists around the world, Malcolm X claimed, ". . . and the reason that they were able to make these gains was they realized that power was the magic word—power against power. Power in defense of freedom is greater than power in behalf of tyranny and oppression, because power, real power, comes from conviction which produces action, uncompromising action. It also produces insurrection against oppression. This is the only way you end oppression—with power."[4] That summer Watts exploded. A year later during the Meredith march in Mississippi, Stokely Carmichael made Black Power the symbol of a new militancy in the struggle for civil rights. In the summer of 1967, following the disturbances in Newark, a national conference on Black Power met in that city in an effort to bring leaders together for more unified action.[5]

Since June 1966, millions of words have been written and spoken on Black Power. The tantalizing ambiguity of the slogan teases forth definition after definition. Asked in a question period following a speech how his definition of Black Power compares with Stokely Carmichael's, Nathan Wright, Jr., author

---

plans to close schools in the ghettos failed for the most part this year, the anniversary of Malcolm's death was observed in several major cities (see "The Beatification of Malcolm X," *Time,* Mar. 1, 1968, p. 16).

[3] "Three Years of Rioting—An Official Record," *U.S. News and World Report,* Nov. 13, 1967, p. 53. These figures were all increased by the outburst in April, 1968, following the murder of Martin Luther King, Jr.

[4] Quoted in Breitman, *op. cit.,* p. 150.

[5] For a summary of the actions of the conference, see "What 'Black Power' Leaders Are Demanding," *U.S. News and World Report,* Aug. 7, 1967, p. 31. For a much more detailed report much less inclined to slant toward the violent actions and overtones, see the reports in *The New York Times* of the conference held on July 20–23, 1967: July 21, p. 1; July 22, p. 1; July 22, p. 11; July 23, p. 18; July 24, p. 1; and July 25, p. 21.

of *Black Power and Urban Unrest: Creative Possibilities*, replied that Carmichael's was Carmichael's and Wright's, Wright's.[6] One is driven to conclude not only that each man has his own meaning for Black Power, but that he has different meanings at different times.

In a series of three essays, Wayne Brockriede and I have argued that the idea of Black Power is open to a constructive interpretation and that although the threat of violence does inhere in the term, those who identify with it most strongly also emphasize an awareness of the power of economic and political unity of the Black community.[7] I would still argue that Black Power is open to an interpretation which is absolutely unobjectionable and totally consistent with democratic ideals. But undeniably the ambiguous phrase, and its users, also show a violent face. I shall address myself here to the nature of the rhetoric of violence that is often expressed under the slogan of Black Power.

Examining the violent rhetoric often associated with militant advocates of Black Power, I draw three conclusions which will be argued in turn. (1) There can be no mistake; we do hear what must be interpreted as the advocacy of violence. (2) The rhetoric of violent Black Power is substantially *justificatory*. Black violence is justified as a response to prior white violence; it is self-defense; as a reaction to racism around the world, it is most readily identified with guerrilla action to overthrow imperialistic colonialism; and it is congruent with the corrupt status quo in America. (3) To maximize the slender hope that may exist for a relatively peaceful, constructive working out of the cry for Black Power, Whites must see the fundamental justification as real. This is not to say simply that Blacks have real grievances but also that the description that justifies is a sensible description of reality that many, perhaps most, Negroes in America experience.

---

[6] See Carroll Greene, "From Riots to Responsibility" (a review of Nathan Wright's *Black Power and Urban Unrest: Creative Possibilities*, New York, Hawthorne Books, Inc., 1967), *Saturday Review*, Aug. 12, 1967, p. 27.

[7] The three essays mentioned are reprinted in this book as Chapters Five, Eight, and Eleven.

I

Many white Americans reading Stokely Carmichael and Charles V. Hamilton's *Black Power: The Politics of Liberation in America* would probably echo the surprise of the book columnist for *Together*, "the Methodist Family Magazine," who described it as a "thoughtful, responsible book that dispels many misconceptions about Black Power."[8] This writer, like the rest of us, had probably seen featured by the news media throughout the summer and fall of 1967 statements Carmichael made during his world tour. For example, he is reported as having "declared coldly" in a message addressed on Radio Havana to Che Guevara, "Yankee Imperialism has existed too long. We are ready to destroy it from the inside. We hope you are ready to destroy it from the outside."[9] This statement is difficult to give a pacific interpretation.

While Carmichael was abroad, his successor as chairman of SNCC, H. Rap Brown, was quoted almost daily in the press. In Cambridge, Maryland, just before a violent outbreak in the ghetto, Brown allegedly shouted, "Black folks built America, and if America don't come around, we're going to burn America down."[10] The next month in Florida, he reportedly advised, "If you are going to loot, brother, loot a gun store. Don't be running around here looting no liquor, 'cause liquor's just for celebrating. . . . You better get yourselves some guns, baby."[11]

In an article entitled "If You Have Any Doubts about Rap Brown Inciting Riots," the *U.S. News and World Report* cited statements like these in making the point the bold headline suggests.[12] Brown, of course, is under indictment in Maryland for inciting a riot. But no matter what degree of innocence or guilt is finally assigned to him, the writer for the *U.S. News* misses the most important aspect of the violent rhetoric of Black Power.

[8] "Looks at New Books," *Together*, February, 1968, p. 64.
[9] *Newsweek*, Aug. 14, 1967, p. 33.
[10] *Newsweek*, Aug. 7, 1967, p. 28.
[11] *Time*, Aug. 18, 1967, p. 21.
[12] Aug. 7, 1967, p. 8. For a much more detailed report of H. Rap Brown's remarks in Cambridge, Md., see *The New York Times*, July 25, 1967, p. 1, and July 26, 1967, p. 1.

II

In concluding his analysis of the forces now working within the ghetto, James Farmer writes, "Ascendency of one camp or the other will be determined ultimately not by rhetoric, and not even by leadership, as much as by events."[13] The relationship between action and the expression of ideas is always difficult to assess, but in this case an assertion of Eric Hoffer's about the role of propaganda may help us: "It penetrates only into minds already open, and rather than instill opinion it articulates and justifies opinions already present in the minds of its recipients."[14] Of course, Hoffer was discussing mass movements in *The True Believer*, and although we can by no means be certain that Black Power represents a mass movement,[15] it certainly bears many of the marks Hoffer singles out.

The rhetoric of violence in Black Power speaking and writing is *justificatory*. Much of it is after-the-fact, clearly explaining violence that has occurred in terms that sanctify. Even that which looks forward to future violence is not so much in the form of recommendation as it is in justification for inevitable acts. It is difficult to say at whom the militant Black Power advocate aims his justificatory arguments. Primarily, they are probably intended to clarify for Black audiences the interpretation the advocate makes of the reality all Blacks share. Secondarily, they may be

[13] "Are White Liberals Obsolete in the Black Struggle?" *Progressive*, January, 1968, p. 16.

[14] *The True Believer*, New York, Harper & Row, Publishers, 1951, p. 103.

[15] "In reality it is a complete myth that Brown as a leader has any base among the masses in the black ghetto. This is not necessarily to his credit, and reflects the reality that his following is primarily among middle class white and black radicals, middle class black nationalists, etc. The same can be said of Stokely Carmichael, who is played into a great black leader not only by the press but by many radicals and socialists as well." Quoted from "H. Rap Brown, Why the Persecution? A Look at His Program," *The Bulletin of International Socialism*, Sept. 11, 1967, p. 1. This statement indicates the dilemma of many socialist organizations which encouraged first the Black Nationalists and now the advocates of Black Power. Since these have insisted on drawing a confrontation of white and black, the socialist doctrine of a class struggle which is strictly economic is left with limited force although many Black Nationalists have explicitly embraced socialism.

meant to spill over to White audiences. Most Whites, of course, hear the messages of violence filtered by the mass media. They seldom hear the justification and almost always hear the calls for violence. We probably ought not believe that the militant aims to convert white listeners; at most, he makes an angry declaration: Now listen, Whitey, this is the way it is!

A key word in the justification of violence is *defense*. This strategic term ought to be easily understood in a nation that witnessed the metamorphosis of a War Department into a Department of Defense and is now engaged in defending freedom-loving peoples everywhere by committing a half million men and thirty-five billion dollars a year in fighting an enemy which is not so much a particular people in a particular place threatening this country directly as it is a symbol of oppression (at least to a majority of Americans).

Defense is nearly always the context when Black Power advocates speak of guns, war, or killing. In an interview in London, Stokely Carmichael is quoted as saying, "In Newark, we applied war tactics of the guerrillas. We are preparing groups of urban guerrillas for our defense in the cities."[16] Self-defense as justification permeates H. Rap Brown's constant talk of guns; for example, he said in a press conference in Washington, D.C., last summer: "I say you better get you a gun. The 'honky' don't respect nothing but guns. He says if he can't kill you in Vietnam he's gonna kill you in the streets of America. And when they get through shooting all the black fellows they're gonna start shooting the black sisters."[17] Malcolm X, whose speeches seem to have given many of the present Black Power advocates numerous leads, emphasized the efficacy of guerrilla warfare against the Whites:

> Nowhere on this earth does the white man win in a guerrilla warfare. It's not his speed. Just as guerrilla warfare is prevailing in Asia and in parts of Africa and in parts of

---

[16] *U.S. News and World Report*, Aug. 7, 1967, p. 32.
[17] *Ibid.*, p. 8. "You got to get the hunkie white man before he gets you." Quoted in *The New York Times*, July 26, 1967, p. 19.

Latin America, you've got to be mighty naive, or you've got to pay the black man cheap, if you don't think some day he's going to wake up and find that it's got to be the ballot or the bullet.[18]

Much of the context in which most of us know guerrilla warfare is one of a just cause—first in this century, the freedom fighters against the Nazis in hundreds of motion pictures and television dramas; next, the revolutions in scores of colonies against imperialist powers. Moreover, Malcolm X's speeches are peppered with references to self-defense.

It is scarcely surprising that Blacks in America have argued theirs as a common cause with colonial revolt around the world. Reminded constantly that they are a minority in the United States, as many spokesmen did early in the debate over Black Power in the summer of 1966,[19] they have made identification with colored peoples around the world a neat reversal of positions and the threat inherent therein. Moreover, colonialism is rather generally accepted as an evil force, and one whose day is done. Colonialism is a symbol of exploitation; resisting such a force is not only just, but success is also inevitable.

Most Whites probably have difficulty thinking of the ghetto as a colony. That label just does not seem to fit. All of this raises the question: How does the Black Power speaker go about making the label seem proper? Perhaps the question itself, no matter how well intentioned, illustrates the deep gulf between the viewpoints of the White liberal and the Black revolutionary. Judging from what the latter says, there is no question. Black people are exploited; colonialism is the means of exploitation; the ghettos are colonies. That line of thought apparently is connection enough to make the symbol a summation of reality. Black Power speakers labeling the ghetto a colony often tick off the White domination of financial and commercial interests in the ghetto and refer often to these in terms that make them

[18] Breitman, *op. cit.*, pp. 37–38.
[19] E.g., Martin Luther King, Jr., at a Chicago rally on July 6, 1966. *Minneapolis Star*, July 7, 1966, p. 3A.

the forces that have supplanted the slave system that brought Blacks to America. Even Martin Luther King, who was quite often referred to as a "flunky" of the white power structure by militants,[20] argued that since the social-economic system is arranged to assure that money flows out without coming back in, the ghettos are colonies.[21]

A constant theme in the analysis of racial unrest in this country is that of the search of the Negro, especially the Negro male, for a positive self-picture, or, to put the matter another way, for a new identity. The "bitter national controversy over proper designation for *identifiable* Americans of African descent," to use Lerone Bennett, Jr.'s description, is an indication of the depth of the problem of identity.[22] Shall these persons refer to themselves as "Negroes," "Blacks," "African-Americans," or "Afro-Americans"? In my opinion, labeling the ghetto as a colony is important in the solution of the "identity crisis" as it is being worked out by militant leaders. Looking at oneself and one's fellows as victims of colonialism provides an explanation for the apathy and ignorance that these Black leaders are often led to denounce, imploring their fellows to be active and intelligent politically. The labels "Black" and, especially, "Afro-American" make a congruent cluster with "colony" and "guerrilla."

A strong sense of *scene* permeates militant Black Power rhetoric. Since Kenneth Burke reminds us that "the scene-act ratio either calls for acts in keeping with scenes or scenes in

[20] See "Black Liberation—Now!" a pamphlet distributed by the Black Liberation Commission of the Progressive Labor Party, 336 Lenox Avenue, Harlem, New York, p. 12.

[21] See "The President's Address to the Tenth Anniversary Convention of the Southern Christian Leadership Conference," Atlanta, Ga., Aug. 16, 1967. (See Chapter Ten, this book.)

[22] "At the Racism in Education Conference of the American Federation of Teachers, the delegates unanimously endorsed a resolution which called on all educators, persons, and organizations to abandon the 'slavery-imposed name' 'Negro' for the terms 'African-American' or 'Afro-American.' A similar resolution was adopted by the Conference on Black Power [Newark, July 20–23, 1967]. But the Black Power conferences compounded the problem by insisting upon the substitution of the word 'Black' for the word 'Negro.'" Quoted from Lerone Bennett, Jr., "What's in a Name? Negro vs. Afro-American vs. Black," *Ebony*, November, 1967, pp. 47–48.

keeping with acts—and similarly with the scene-agent ratio,"[23] we would be well advised to try to see the scene as the Black Power militants tend to.

As one might expect, violence against Negroes is constantly featured in Black Power rhetoric. The effect, however, is not simply to argue that these acts are unjust and that the existence of certain human rights demands action and redress. There is a larger impact, that of a violent milieu, one that breeds violence, one in which a man must be violent. Dwelling on the violence of kidnapping and transporting Blacks to the plantation economy run by violence and tracing the migration of Blacks from the violent post-reconstruction Southern reaction to the brutality of ghetto life in the North pictures an inescapable heritage of violence.

Such scene painting demands the stark simple figure of an enemy. The rhetoric of militant Black Power answers the demand. The disrespectful terms that lump together all non-Blacks are familiar to every alert American. Not only do we hear repeatedly the terms "honky" and "whitey," but we catch the different tone and context for uttering "the man." What that term personifies has shifted dramatically. "The man" *was* he on whom the Negro depended and to whom he had to defer; "the man" *is* all of White society on which the Afro-American asserts he will not depend and to which he will not defer. White society is all of a piece to the militant. As H. Rap Brown shouted in Cambridge, Maryland, "When the Klan gets together to kill a nigger, they just kill anyone they see walking down the street. And the Klan thinks like white folk in America, brother."[24]

Many Black Power advocates feel that they have been sold out and tricked repeatedly by Whites when they have tried to use peaceful, democratic means. This contention is apparent even in the moderate book on Black Power by Carmichael and Hamilton.[25] In describing the formation of the Black Panther

[23] *A Grammar of Motives*, Englewood, N.J., Prentice-Hall, Inc., 1945, p. 9.
[24] *The New York Times*, July 25, 1967, p. 20.
[25] See, especially, "Mississippi Freedom Democrats: Bankruptcy of the Establishment," Chap. 4 in *Black Power: The Politics of Liberation in America*, New York, Random House, Inc., 1967.

Party, John Hulett, chairman of the Lowndes County [Alabama] Freedom Organization, in a speech in Los Angeles recounts bitterly the "racist tricks" his group faced.[26] Not surprisingly, H. Rap Brown sees the forces arrayed against him as conspiratorial.[27] Many, like Brown, see all talk of integration and cooperation as "tokenism" at best and usually as transparent attempts to keep the Black citizen subjugated. Negroes who argue for nonviolence and integration are pictured as stooges of the White power structure. So thoroughly have the militants denounced those who cooperate with Whites, thus using the support of the White power structure as a basis of their influence, that "leader" and especially "Negro leader" have become negative terms. In a speech before a Black audience in Detroit, Stokely Carmichael was quick to say, "We have a lot of Negro leaders, and I want to make it clear that I'm no leader."[28]

Although most well-intentioned Whites who are willing to think critically can see the merit of the argument that much White participation in the civil rights fight did tend to suggest a subtle sort of racism, that is, the superiority of the helpers over those to be helped, this ground alone seems much too little to account for the bitterness of the denunciation of "White liberals" found in much Black Power speaking and writing.[29] Seen in the light of a rhetoric justifying violence, however, that aspect of Black Power rhetoric is more easily understood. The view of an exploitative, conspiratorial, unified enemy demanded by the rationale of the ghetto as a colony justifying guerrilla warfare in self-defense cannot accommodate the experience of well-motivated Whites unstintingly dedicated to eradicating the oppressive conditions. The paradox of a political party which contains both the most obviously segregationist power of America together with those who claim to be the liberal friends of the Blacks is

[26] See "How the Black Panther Party Was Organized," in *The Black Panther Party*, New York, Merit Publishers, 1966, pp. 7–15.

[27] See *U.S. News and World Report*, Aug. 7, 1967, p. 8.

[28] Speech in Cobo Auditorium, July 30, 1966. (See Chapter Six, this book.)

[29] For a discussion of the resentment of white civil rights workers by many Negroes in "the movement," see Alvin F. Poussaint, "How the 'White Problem' Spawned 'Black Power,'" *Ebony*, August, 1967, pp. 88–94.

difficult to comprehend at best. In the face of continued failure to make anything but token progress, a ready explanation is that fundamentally the Northern liberals and segregationist Southerners share the necessity of keeping Blacks subjugated.

Having returned from abroad, Malcolm X told an audience about learning from some Algerians how they made Frenchmen who came to them saying, "We're with you" prove their loyalty. "I won't tell you what the test was, but they put them to the test."[30] For many Negroes, the test for the White liberal was the demand to pull the Democratic party apart if necessary. The failure of the 1964 convention to seat the delegates sent by the Mississippi Freedom Democrats was the act that proved that at bottom the interests of all Whites are alike. In that act, White liberals professing the welfare of Blacks are revealed as conspirators, more dangerous than open segregationists, since they mask their motives. The very presence of many Whites in civil rights actions can be taken as admission of a feeling of guilt engendered by the racist nature of American society. All Whites are contaminated by racist guilt.

"Hatred is the most accessible and comprehensive of all unifying agents," Eric Hoffer concludes.[31] There can be little doubt that the militant advocates of Black Power are seeking Black unity. All calls for unity of a group will suggest that those not of the group are to be disdained or mistrusted or feared and often hated. Hatred engenders hatred. It is difficult to hate by half measures. It is easy to hate if one can blame others for the conditions that create hatred.

Frantz Fanon, the African-born, French-educated psychiatrist who became a revolutionary theorist during the Algerian rebellion, has become a prophet for militant Afro-Americans. Fanon continually pictures the world created by the European colonists as Manichean. The justification of colonialism as a civilizing force cast the native in the role of evil to be overcome, something not yet human threatening to engulf the good represented by the Whites. In such a world the native is forced to struggle;

[30] Quoted in Breitman, *op. cit.*, p. 71.
[31] Hoffer, *op. cit.*, p. 89.

it is not a struggle he can win by peaceful means because he himself needs transformation. He has been subjugated, not simply physically exploited, but psychologically devalued. "At the level of individuals," Fanon wrote, "violence is a cleansing force. It frees the native from his inferiority complex and from his despair and inaction; it makes him fearless and restores his self-respect."[32]

## III

The analytic weakness of taking Black Power militants as inciting riots is that the problem is reduced to that of a few criminals bringing about action that would otherwise probably not be forthcoming. Such an analysis suggests that the remedy is ordinary legal action, invoking the clear sanctions of society in defense of society. I am obviously in no position to judge the actions of any of the principals on the legal criteria of incitement. Whether or not H. Rap Brown or any other militant Black Power advocate ought to be convicted of such a charge seems to me secondary to the reading of their rhetoric as justificatory. I believe that we must assume that their rhetoric makes clear the world as it is for many, perhaps most, Black Americans. The ghetto is a colony; the White is the enemy; a racist society is violent.

Police Chief Kinnamon of Cambridge, Maryland, concluded that his community suffered "a well-planned Communist attempt to overthrow the city government."[33] If like Mr. Kinnamon, we seek scapegoats outside ourselves, we shall probably compound the serious difficulties we face. We need not doubt that Communists seek to profit from social upheaval in this country. But neither do we need to doubt that the Black militants have seen one of the true faces of reality in this country and that what they have seen is more important than any foreign exploitation of the circumstances.

[32] *The Wretched of the Earth,* trans. by Constance Farrington, New York, Grove Press, Inc., 1963, p. 73.
[33] *Newsweek,* Aug. 7, 1967, p. 28.

Truth in a social sense is always created by the human beings who participate in its articulation. What at least a few members of a Black minority see as truth, they see permeating the reality of America. If we face this truth, we may be able to participate in building fresh truth, or in re-valuing some old but fundamental American axioms. Personally, I am *not* optimistic, but as the psychiatrist Fanon mentions looking at African revolutions, violence can be worked out symbolically.[34] Malcolm X did feature the alternative of the ballot or the bullet.

We ought to have no illusions. It will make no difference whether or not we accept the reality of Black militant rhetoric; the outcome of our racial conflicts in any case will be revolutionary. "The natives are convinced that their fate is in the balance, here and now," Fanon wrote. "They live in the atmosphere of doomsday. . . ."[35] So does the militant advocate of Black Power. And so do we all. Discussing the "principle of escalation" in his plans for the revolt last fall at San Jose State College, the militant professor Harry Edwards said, "If anyone had touched us, we would have sent him to the cemetery."[36]

If matters come to numerous pitched battles, White Power may be able to eradicate Black Power. But pacification of our Black citizens will destroy America as surely as the worst imagining of any Communist takeover. At that moment the remnants of a rational, open, democratic society will be destroyed. The segregationist dream of a contented, dependent, deferential Black minority can be accomplished only in a police state. And it will be a police state for us all.

A relatively peaceful working out of Black Power may often seem a dim hope, but it is the only sensible hope for which Americans can work. This is why we must insist on political and economic power for united Black communities. Stokely Carmichael and other militant Blacks have argued repeatedly that coalitions of White groups and Black are possible *after*

---

[34] Fanon, *op. cit.*, pp. 73–74.

[35] *Ibid.*, p. 63.

[36] Quoted in James Brann, "San Jose: The Bullhorn Message," *The Nation*, Nov. 6, 1967, p. 466.

Negroes have gained real economic and political power.[37] White America ought to take them at their word. To fail to do so will be to accept a violent working out of Black Power and its inevitable consequences.

[37] See, for example, "The Myths of Coalition," Chap. 3 in Carmichael and Hamilton's *Black Power*.

## CHAPTER TEN

# The President's Address to the Tenth Anniversary Convention of the Southern Christian Leadership Conference, Atlanta, Georgia, August 16, 1967

*Martin Luther King, Jr.*

There are many similarities between this speech by Martin Luther King, Jr., delivered to the organization that was one of the products of the Montgomery bus boycott in 1956, and the description of Black Power in Chapter Three. This is scarcely surprising. But we can also see in comparing the two the direction in which King's thought was developing. In a sense, his proposal of a Poor People's March was a response to the division that in his eyes threatened the reforms essential to bringing this nation closer to true democracy.

Dr. Abernathy, our distinguished Vice President, fellow delegates to this Tenth Annual session of the Southern Christian Leadership Conference, my brothers and sisters from not only all over the South, but from all over the United States of America:

Ten years ago, during the piercing chill of a January day and on the heels of the year-long Montgomery bus boycott, a group of approximately 100 Negro leaders from across the South assembled in this church and agreed on the need for an organization to be formed that could serve as a channel through which local protest organizations in the South could co-ordinate their protest activities. It was this meeting that gave birth to the Southern Christian Leadership Conference.

SOURCE: This address is reprinted by special arrangement with the SCLC, Atlanta, Ga.

When our organization was formed ten years ago, racial segregation was still a structured part of the architecture of Southern society. Negroes with the pangs of hunger and anguish of thirst were denied access to the average lunch counter. The downtown restaurants were still off limits for the black man. Negroes, burdened with the fatigue of travel, were still barred from the motels of the highways and the hotels of the cities. Negro boys and girls in dire need of recreational activities were not allowed to inhale the fresh air of the big city parks. Negroes in desperate need of allowing their mental buckets to sink deep into the wells of knowledge were confronted with a firm "no" when they sought to use the city libraries. Ten years ago, legislative halls of the South were still ringing loud with such words as "interposition" and "nullification." All types of conniving methods were still being used to keep the Negro from becoming a registered voter. A decade ago, not a single Negro entered the legislative chambers of the South except as a porter or chauffeur. Ten years ago, all too many Negroes were still harried by day and haunted by night by a corroding sense of fear and a nagging sense of "nobodyness."

But things are different now. In assault after assault, we caused the sagging walls of segregation to come tumbling down. During this era the entire edifice of segregation was profoundly shaken. This is an accomplishment whose consequences are deeply felt by every Southern Negro in his daily life. It is no longer possible to count the number of public establishments that are open to Negroes. Ten years ago, Negroes seemed almost invisible to the larger society, and the facts of their harsh lives were unknown to the majority of the nation. But today, Civil Rights is a dominating issue in every state, crowding the pages of the press and the daily conversation of white Americans. In this decade of change, the Negro stood up and confronted his oppressor. He faced the bullies and the guns, the dogs and the tear gas. He put himself squarely before the vicious mobs and moved with strength and dignity toward them and decisively defeated them. The courage with which he confronted enraged mobs dissolved the stereotype of the grinning, submissive Uncle Tom. He came out of his struggle integrated only slightly in the external society, but powerfully integrated within. This was a victory that had to precede all other gains.

In short, over the last ten years, the Negro decided to straighten his back up, realizing that a man cannot ride your back unless it is bent. We made our government write new laws to alter some of the cruelest injustices that affected us. We made an indifferent and unconcerned nation arise from lethargy and subpoena its conscience to appear before the judgment seat of morality on the whole question of Civil Rights. We gained manhood in the nation that had always called us "boy." It would be hypocritical indeed if I allowed modesty to forbid my saying that SCLC stood at the forefront of all of the watershed movements that brought about these monumental changes in the South. For this, we can feel a legitimate pride. But, despite a decade of significant progress, the problem is far from solved.

The deep rumbling of discontent in our cities is indicative of the fact that the plant of freedom has grown only a bud and not yet a flower.

Before discussing the awesome responsibilities that we face in the days ahead, let us take an inventory of our programmatic action and activities over the past year. Last year as we met in Jackson, Mississippi, we were painfully aware of the struggle of our brothers in Grenada, Mississippi. After living for a hundred or more years under the yoke of total segregation, Negro citizens of this Northern Delta hamlet banded together in nonviolent warfare against racial discrimination under the leadership of our affiliated chapter and organization there. That this nondestructive rebellion occurred was as spectacular as were its results. In a few short weeks the Grenada County Freedom Movement challenged every aspect of the society's exploitive life: Stores which denied employment were boycotted, and Voter Registration increased by thousands. We can never forget the courageous action of the people of Grenada who moved our nation and its federal courts to powerful action in behalf of school integration, giving Grenada one of the most integrated school systems in America. The battle is far from over, but the black people of Grenada have achieved 40 of 53 demands through their persistent nonviolent efforts.

Slowly but surely, our Southern affiliates continued their building and organizing. Seventy-nine counties conducted voter registration drives, while double that number carried on political education and get-out-the-vote efforts. Despite press opinions, our staff is still overwhelmingly a Southern-based staff. One hundred and five persons have worked across the South under the direction of Hosea Williams. What used to be primarily a voter registration staff is actually a multifaceted program dealing with the total life of the community, including farm co-operatives, business development, tutorials, and credit unions. Especially to be commended are those 99 communities and their staffs which maintain regular mass meetings throughout the year.

Our Citizenship Education Program continues to lay the solid foundation for adult education and community organization upon which all social change must ultimately rest. This year, 500 local leaders received training at Dorchester and ten community centers through our Citizenship Education Program. They were trained in literacy, consumer education, planned parenthood, and many other things. This program, so ably directed by Mrs. Dorothy Cotton, Mrs. Septima Clark and their staff of eight persons, continues to cover ten Southern States. An auxiliary feature of C. E. P. is the aid given to poor communities and counties in receiving and establishing O. E. O. projects. With the competent professional guidance of our marvelous staff member, Miss Mew Soong-Li, Lowndes and Wilcox Counties in Alabama have pioneered in developing outstanding poverty programs totally controlled and operated by residents of the area.

Perhaps the area of greatest concentration of my efforts has been in the cities of Chicago and Cleveland. Chicago has been a wonderful proving ground for our work in the North. There have been no earth-shaking victories, but neither have there been failures. Our open-housing marches, which finally brought about an agreement, actually caused the power structure of Chicago to capitulate to the Civil Rights Movement. These marches and the agreement have finally begun to pay off. After a season of delay during the election periods, a Leadership Conference, which was organized in Chicago to meet our demands for an open city, has finally begun to implement the programs agreed upon last summer. But this is not the most important aspect of our work. As a result of our tenant-union organizing, we have begun a 4-million-dollar rehabilitation project which will renovate deteriorating buildings and give the tenants the opportunity to own their own homes. This pilot project was the inspiration for the new home-ownership bill which Senator Percy introduced in Congress only recently.

The most dramatic success in Chicago has been Operation Breadbasket. Through Operation Breadbasket we have now achieved for the Negro community of Chicago more than 2,200 new jobs worth approximately 18 million dollars a year in new income to the Negro community. Not only have we gotten jobs through Operation Breadbasket in Chicago; there is another operational area in this economic program, involving the development of Negro-controlled financial institutions which are sensitive to the problems of economic deprivation in Negro communities. The two banks in Chicago that were interested in helping Negro businessmen were largely unable to loan much money because of limited assets. Several chain stores in Chicago agreed to maintain substantial accounts in the two banks, thus increasing their ability to serve the needs of the Negro community. And I can say to you today, that as a result of Operation Breadbasket in Chicago both of these Negro-operated banks have now more than doubled their assets—and this has been accomplished in less than a year!

In addition, the Breadbasket ministers learned that Negro scavengers had been deprived of significant accounts in the ghetto. Whites controlled even the garbage of Negroes. Consequently, the chain stores agreed to contract with Negro scavengers to service at least the stores in Negro areas. Previously, Negro insect and rodent exterminators, as well as janitorial services, were likewise excluded from major contracts with chain stores. The chain stores also agreed to utilize these services. It also became apparent that chain stores advertised only rarely in Negro-owned newspapers. This area of neglect was also negotiated, giving community newspapers regular, substantial advertising income. Indeed, the ministers found that almost *all* contractors, from painters to masons, from electricians to excavators had also been forced to remain small by the monopolies of white contractors. Breadbasket negotiated agreements on new construction and rehabilitation work for the chain stores. These inter-related aspects of economic development, all based on the power of the organized consumer, hold great possibilities for dealing with the problems of Negroes in other Northern cities. The kinds of requests made by Breadbasket in Chicago can be made not only of chain stores but of almost any major industry in any other city in the country. So, Operation Breadbasket has a very simple program but a powerful one. It simply says, "If you respect my dollar, you must respect my person." It simply says, "We will no longer spend our money where we cannot get substantial jobs."

In Cleveland, Ohio, a group of ministers have formed an Operation Breadbasket through our program there and have moved against a major dairy company. Their requests include jobs, advertising in Negro newspapers and depositing funds in Negro financial institutions. This effort resulted in something marvelous. I went to Cleveland just last week to sign the agreement with Sealtest. We went to get the facts about their employment. We discovered that they had 442 employees and only 43 were Negroes. And yet, the Negro population of Cleveland is 35% of the total population. They refused to give us all of the information that we requested and we said in substance, "Mr. Sealtest, we are sorry. We aren't going to throw any bricks in the window. But we are going to put picket signs up, and we are going to pass out leaflets and we are going to our pulpits to tell them not to sell or purchase Sealtest products." We did just that. We went through the churches. The Reverend Dr. Hoover who pastors the largest church in Cleveland, and who is here today, and all of the ministers, got together and got behind this program. We went to every store in the ghetto and said, "You must take Sealtest products off your counters. If not, we're going to boycott your whole store." A & P refused. We put picket lines around A & P. They have more than 100 stores in Cleveland. And we picketed A & P and closed down 18 of them in one day. Nobody went to the A & P.

The next day, Mr. A & P was calling on us, and Bob Brown, who is on our Board and who is a public relations man representing a number of firms, came in. They called him in because he works for A & P also and they didn't know he worked for us, too. Bob Brown sat down with A & P and they said, "Now Mr. Brown, what would you advise us to do?" He said, "I would advise you to take Sealtest products off all of your counters." A & P agreed next day not only to take Sealtest products off the counters in the ghetto but off the counters of every A & P store in Cleveland and they said to Sealtest, "If you don't reach an agreement with SCLC and Operation Breadbasket, we will take Sealtest products out of every A & P store in the State of Ohio tomorrow." The next day, the Sealtest people were talking nice. They were very humble. And I am proud to say that I went to Cleveland just last Tuesday and I sat down with the Sealtest people and some 70 ministers from Cleveland and we signed the agreement and this effort resulted in a number of jobs which will bring almost $500,000 a year in new income to the Negro community.

We also said to Sealtest, "The problem that we face is that the ghetto is a domestic colony that's constantly drained without being replenished. You are always telling us to lift ourselves by our own bootstraps and yet we are being robbed every day. Put something back in the ghetto!" So along with our demand for jobs we said, "We also demand that you put money in the Negro Savings and Loan Association and that you advertise in the Cleveland *Call and Post,* the Negro newspaper." So along with the new jobs, Sealtest has now deposited thousands of dollars in the Negro bank of Cleveland and has already started taking ads in the Negro newspaper in that city. This is the power of Operation Breadbasket.

Now, for fear you may think this is limited to Chicago and Cleveland, let me say to you that we have achieved more than that in Atlanta, Georgia. Breadbasket has been equally successful in the South. Here, the emphasis has been divided between governmental employment and private industry. And while I do not have the time to go into the details, I want to commend the men who have been working with it here: The Reverends Fred

C. Bennette, Joseph Boone, J. C. Ward, E. H. Dorsey, J. D. Grier, and I could go on down the line. They have stood up along with all the other ministers. But here is the story that is not printed in the newspapers in Atlanta. As a result of Operation Breadbasket, over the last three years, we have added about 25 million dollars in new income to the Negro community every year.

Now, as you know, Operation Breadbasket has gone national, in the sense that we had a conference in Chicago and agreed to launch a nation-wide program which you will hear more about.

Finally, SCLC has entered the field of housing. Under the leadership of Attorney James Robinson, we have already contracted to build 152 units of low-income housing with apartments for the elderly on a choice downtown Atlanta site, under the sponsorship of Ebenezer Baptist Church. This is the first project in a proposed South-wide housing development corporation which we hope to develop in conjunction with SCLC. Through this corporation, we hope to build housing from Mississippi to North Carolina using Negro workmen, Negro architects, Negro attorneys, and Negro financial institutions throughout. And it is our feeling that in the next two or three years we can build, right here in the South, 40 million dollars worth of new housing for Negroes, with millions and millions of dollars in income to the Negro community.

Now there are many other things that I could tell you, but time is passing. This, in short, is an account of SCLC's work over the last year. It is a record of which we can all be proud.

With all the struggle and all the achievements, however, we must face the fact that the Negro still lives in the basement of the Great Society. He is still at the bottom despite the few who have penetrated to slightly higher levels. Even where the door has been forced partially open, mobility for the Negro is still sharply restricted. There is often no bottom from which to start. And where there is, there is almost no room at the top. Consequently, Negroes are still impoverished aliens in an affluent society. They are too poor even to rise with the society, too impoverished by the ages to be able to ascend by using their own resources. The Negro did not do this to himself. It was done to him. For more than half of his American history, he was enslaved. Yet he built the spanning bridges, the grand mansions, the sturdy docks and stout factories of the South. His unpaid labor made cotton a king, and established America as a significant nation in international commerce. Even after his release from chattel slavery, the nation grew over him, submerging him. America became the richest, most powerful society in the history of man. But it left the Negro far behind. So we still have a long, long way to go before we reach the promised land of freedom. Yes, we have left the dusty soils of Egypt. We have crossed the Red Sea that had for years been hardened by the long and piercing winters of passive resistance. Before we reach the majestic shores of the promised land there will still be gigantic mountains of opposition ahead and prodigious hilltops of injustice. We still need some Paul Reveres of conscience to alert every hamlet and every village of America that revolution is at hand. Yes, we need a chart. We need a compass. Indeed we need some North Star to guide us into a future shrouded with impenetrable uncertainties.

Now, in order to answer the question, "Where do we go from here?" which is our theme, we must first honestly recognize where we are now. When the Constitution was written a strange formula to determine taxes and representation declared that the Negro was 60% of a person. Today another curious formula seems to declare he is 50% of a person. Of the good things in life, the Negro has approximately one-half those of whites. Of the bad things of life, he has twice those of whites. Thus half of all Negroes live in substandard housing. And Negroes have half the income of whites. When we view the negative experiences of life, the Negro has a double share. There are twice as many unemployed. The rate of infant mortality among Negroes is double that of whites and there are twice as many Negroes dying in Vietnam as whites in proportion to their size in the population.

In other spheres, the figures are equally alarming. In elementary schools, Negroes lag one to three years behind whites and their segregated schools receive substantially less money per student than the white schools. One-twentieth as many Negroes as whites attend college. Of employed Negroes, 75% hold menial jobs.

This is where we are—Where do we go from here? First, we must massively assert our dignity and worth. We must stand up amidst a system that still oppresses us and develop an unassailable and majestic sense of values. We must no longer be ashamed of being black. The job of arousing manhood within a people that have been taught for so many centuries that they are nobody is not easy.

Even semantics have conspired to make that which is black seem ugly and degrading. In Roget's Thesaurus there are 120 synonyms for blackness and at least 60 of them are offensive, as for example, blot, soot, grim, devil and foul. And there are some 134 synonyms for whiteness and all are favorable, expressed in such words as purity, cleanliness, chastity and innocence. A white lie is better than a black lie. The most degenerate member of a family is a "black sheep." Ossie Davis has suggested that maybe the English language should be reconstructed so that teachers will not be forced to teach the Negro child 60 ways to despise himself, and thereby perpetuate his false sense of inferiority, and the white child 134 ways to adore himself, and thereby perpetuate his false sense of superiority.

The tendency to ignore the Negro's contribution to American life and to strip him of his personhood, is as old as the earliest history books and as contemporary as the morning's newspaper. To upset this cultural homicide, the Negro must rise up with an affirmation of his own Olympian manhood. Any movement for the Negro's freedom that overlooks this necessity is only waiting to be buried. As long as the mind is enslaved, the body can never be free. Psychological freedom, a firm sense of self-esteem, is the most powerful weapon against the long night of physical slavery. No Lincolnian Emancipation Proclamation or Johnsonian Civil Rights Bill can totally bring this kind of freedom. The Negro will only be free when he reaches down to the inner depths of his own being and signs with the pen and ink of assertive manhood his own Emancipation Proclamation. And, with a spirit straining toward true self-esteem, the Negro must boldly throw off the manacles of self-abnegation and say to him-

self and to the world, "I am somebody. I am a person. I am a
man with dignity and honor. I have a rich and noble history.
How painful and exploited that history has been. Yes, I was a
slave through my foreparents and I am not ashamed of that.
I'm ashamed of the people who were so sinful to make me a
slave." Yes, we must stand up and say, "I'm black and I'm
beautiful," and this self-affirmation is the black man's need,
made compelling by the white man's crimes against him.

Another basic challenge is to discover how to organize our
strength in terms of economic and political power. No one can
deny that the Negro is in dire need of this kind of legitimate
power. Indeed, one of the great problems that the Negro confronts is his lack of power. From old plantations of the South
to newer ghettos of the North, the Negro has been confined to a
life of voicelessness and powerlessness. Stripped of the right to
make decisions concerning his life and destiny he has been
subject to the authoritarian and sometimes whimsical decisions
of this white power structure. The plantation and ghetto were
created by those who had power, both to confine those who had
no power and to perpetuate their powerlessness. The problem of
transforming the ghetto, therefore, is a problem of power: A
confrontation of the forces of power demanding change and the
forces of power dedicated to the preserving of the status quo.
Now power properly understood is nothing but the ability to
achieve purpose. It is the strength required to bring about social,
political, and economic change. Walter Reuther defined power
one day. He said, "Power is the ability of a labor union like the
U.A.W. to make the most powerful corporation in the world,
General Motors, say 'yes' when it wants to say 'no.' That's
power."

Now a lot of us are preachers, and all of us have our moral
convictions and concerns, and so often have problems with
power. There is nothing wrong with power if power is used
correctly. You see, what happened is that some of our philoso-
phers got off base. And one of the great problems of history is
that the concepts of love and power have usually been contrasted
as opposites—polar opposites—so that love is identified with a
resignation of power, and power with a denial of love.

It was this misinterpretation that caused Nietzsche, who was a philosopher of the will to power, to reject the Christian concept of love. It was this same misinterpretation which induced Christian theologians to reject the Nietzschian philosophy of the will to power in the name of the Christian idea of love. Now, we've got to get this thing right. What is needed is a realization that power without love is reckless and abusive and love without power is sentimental and anemic. Power at its best is love implementing the demands of justice, and justice at its best is power correcting everything that stands against love. And this is what we must see as we move on. What has happened is that we have had it wrong and confused in our own country, and this has led Negro Americans in the past to seek their goals through power devoid of love and conscience.

This is leading a few extremists today to advocate for Negroes the same destructive and conscienceless power that they have justly abhorred in whites. It is precisely this collision of immoral power with powerless morality which constitutes the major crisis of our times.

We must develop a program that will drive the nation to a guaranteed annual income. Now, early in this century this proposal would have been greeted with ridicule and denunciation, as destructive of initiative and responsibility. At that time economic status was considered the measure of the individual's ability and talents. And, in the thinking of that day, the absence of worldly goods indicated a want of industrious habits and moral fiber. We've come a long way in our understanding of human motivation and of the blind operation of our economic system. Now we realize that dislocations in the market operations of our economy and the prevalence of discrimination thrust people into idleness and bind them in constant or frequent unemployment against their will. Today the poor are less often dismissed, I hope, from our consciences by being branded as inferior or incompetent. We also know that no matter how dynamically the economy develops and expands, it does not eliminate all poverty.

The problem indicates that our emphasis must be two-fold. We must create full employment or we must create incomes.

People must be made consumers by one method or the other. Once they are placed in this position we need to be concerned that the potential of the individual is not wasted. New forms of work that enhance the social good will have to be devised for those for whom traditional jobs are not available. In 1879 Henry George anticipated this state of affairs when he wrote in *Progress and Poverty:*

"The fact is that the work which improves the condition of mankind, the work which extends knowledge and increases power and enriches literature and elevates thought, is not done to secure a living. It is not the work of slaves driven to their tasks either by the task, by the taskmaster, or by animal necessity. It is the work of men who somehow find a form of work that brings a security for its own sake and a state of society where want is abolished."

Work of this sort could be enormously increased, and we are likely to find that the problems of housing and education, instead of preceding the elimination of poverty, will themselves be affected if poverty is first abolished. The poor transformed into purchasers will do a great deal on their own to alter housing decay. Negroes who have a double disability will have a greater effect on discrimination when they have the additional weapon of cash to use in their struggle.

Beyond these advantages, a host of positive psychological changes inevitably will result from widespread economic security. The dignity of the individual will flourish when the decisions concerning his life are in his own hands, when he has the means to seek self-improvement. Personal conflicts among husbands, wives, and children will diminish when the unjust measurement of human worth on the scale of dollars is eliminated.

Now our country can do this. John Kenneth Galbraith said that a guaranteed annual income could be done for about 20 billion dollars a year. And I say to you today, that if our nation can spend 35 billion dollars a year to fight an unjust, evil war in Vietnam, and 20 billion dollars to put a man on the moon, it can spend billions of dollars to put God's children on their own two feet right here on earth.

Now, let me say briefly that we must reaffirm our commitment to nonviolence. I want to stress this. The futility of violence in the struggle for racial justice has been tragically etched in all the recent Negro riots. Yesterday, I tried to analyze the riots and deal with their causes. Today I want to give the other side. There is certainly something painfully sad about a riot. One sees screaming youngsters and angry adults fighting hopelessly and aimlessly against impossible odds. And deep down within them, you can even see a desire for self-destruction, a kind of suicidal longing.

Occasionally Negroes contend that the 1965 Watts riot and the other riots in various cities represented effective civil rights action. But those who express this view always end up with stumbling words when asked what concrete gains have been won as a result. At best, the riots have produced a little additional anti-poverty money allotted by frightened government officials, and a few water-sprinklers to cool the children of the ghettos. It is something like improving the food in the prison while the people remain securely incarcerated behind bars. Nowhere have the riots won any concrete improvement such as have the organized protest demonstrations. When one tries to pin down advocates of violence as to what acts could be effective, the answers are blatantly illogical. Sometimes they talk of overthrowing racist state and local governments and they talk about guerrilla warfare. They fail to see that no internal revolution has ever succeeded in overthrowing a government by violence unless the government had already lost the allegiance and effective control of its armed forces. Anyone in his right mind knows that this will not happen in the United States. In a violent racial situation, the power structure has the local Police, the State Troopers, the National Guard and, finally, the Army to call on—all of which are predominantly white. Furthermore, few if any violent revolutions have been successful unless the violent minority had the sympathy and support of the non-resistant majority. Castro may have had only a few Cubans actually fighting with him up in the hills, but he could never have overthrown the Batista regime unless he had the sympathy of the vast majority of Cuban people.

It is perfectly clear that a violent revolution on the part of American blacks would find no sympathy and support from the white population and very little from the majority of the Negroes themselves. This is no time for romantic illusions and empty philosophical debates about freedom. This is a time for action. What is needed is a strategy for change, a tactical program that will bring the Negro into the mainstream of American life as quickly as possible. So far, this has only been offered by the nonviolent movement. Without recognizing this we will end up with solutions that don't solve, answers that don't answer and explanations that don't explain.

And so I say to you today that I still stand by nonviolence. And I am still convinced that it is the most potent weapon available to the Negro in his struggle for justice in this country. And the other thing is that I am concerned about a better world. I'm concerned about justice. I'm concerned about brotherhood. I'm concerned about truth. And when one is concerned about these, he can never advocate violence. For through violence you may murder a murderer but you can't murder, murder. Through violence you may murder a liar but you can't establish truth. Through violence you may murder a hater, but you can't murder hate. Darkness cannot put out darkness. Only light can do that.

And I say to you, I have also decided to stick to love. For I know that love is ultimately the only answer to mankind's problems. And I'm going to talk about it everywhere I go. I know it isn't popular to talk about it in some circles today. I'm not talking about emotional bosh when I talk about love, I'm talking about a strong, demanding love. And I have seen too much hate. I've seen too much hate on the faces of sheriffs in the South. I've seen hate on the faces of too many Klansmen and too many White Citizen's Councilors in the South to want to hate myself, because every time I see it, I know that it does something to their faces and their personalities and I say to myself that hate is too great a burden to bear. I have decided to love. If you are seeking the highest good, I think you can find it through love. And the beautiful thing is that we are moving against wrong when we do it, because John was right, God is love. He who hates does not know God, but he who has love has the key that unlocks the door to the meaning of ultimate reality.

And so I say to you today my friends, that you may be able to speak with the tongues of men and angels. You may have the eloquence of articulate speech, but if you have not love, it means nothing. Yes, you may have the gift of prophecy, you may have the gift of scientific prediction and understand the behavior of molecules. You may break into the storehouse of nature and bring forth many new insights. Yes, you may ascend to the heights of academic achievement so that you have all knowledge. And you may boast of your great institutions of learning and boundless extent of your degrees, but if you have not love, all of these mean absolutely nothing. You may even give of your goods to feed the poor. You may bestow great gifts to charity. You may tower high in philanthropy. But, if you have not love, your charity means nothing. You may even give your body to be burned and die the death of a martyr, and your spilled blood may be a symbol of honor for generations yet unborn, and thousands may praise you as one of history's greatest heroes. But, if you have not love, your blood was spilt in vain. What I am trying to get you to see this morning is that a man may be self-centered in his self-denial and self-righteous in his self-sacrifice. His generosity may feed his ego and his piety may feed his pride. So, without love, benevolence becomes egotism and martyrdom becomes spiritual pride.

I want to say to you as I move to my conclusion, as we talk about "Where do we go from here," that we must honestly face the fact that the Movement must address itself to the question of restructuring the whole of American society. There are 40 million poor people here. And one day we must ask the question, "Why are there 40 million poor people in America?" And when you begin to ask that question, you are raising questions about the economic system, about a broader distribution of wealth. When you ask that question, you begin to question the capitalistic economy. And I'm simply saying that more and more, we've got to begin to ask questions about the whole society. We are called upon to help the discouraged beggars in life's market place. But one day we must come to see that an edifice which produces beggars needs restructuring. It means that questions must be raised. You see, my friends, when you deal with this, you begin to ask the question, "Who owns the oil?" You begin to ask the question, "Who owns the iron ore?" You begin to ask the question, "Why is it that people have to pay water bills in a world that is two-thirds water?" These are questions that must be asked.

Now, don't think that you have me in a "bind" today. I'm not talking about Communism. What I'm talking about is far beyond Communism. My inspiration didn't come from Karl Marx. My inspiration didn't come from Engels. My inspiration didn't come from Trotsky. My inspiration didn't come from Lenin. Yes, I read *The Communist Manifesto* and *Das Kapital* a long time ago. And I saw that maybe Marx didn't follow Hegel enough. He took his dialectics, but he left out his idealism and his spiritualism, and he went over to a German philosopher by the name of Feuerbach and took his materialism and made it into a system that he called dialectical materialism. I have to reject that.

What I'm saying to you this morning is that Communism forgets that life is individual. Capitalism forgets that life is social, and the Kingdom of Brotherhood is found neither in the thesis of Communism nor the antithesis of Capitalism but in a higher synthesis. It is found in a higher synthesis that combines the truths of both. Now, when I say question the whole society, it means ultimately coming to see that the problem of racism, the problem of economic exploitation, and the problem of war are all tied together. These are the triple evils that are interrelated.

If you will let me be a preacher just a little bit: One night, a juror came to Jesus and he wanted to know what he could do to be saved. Jesus didn't get bogged down in the kind of isolated approach of what he shouldn't do. Jesus didn't say, "Now Nicodemus, you must stop lying." He didn't say, "Nicodemus, you must stop cheating if you are doing that." He didn't say, "Nicodemus, you must not commit adultery." He didn't say, "Nicodemus, now you must stop drinking liquor if you are doing that excessively." He said something altogether different, because Jesus realized something basic—that if a man will lie, he will steal. And if a man will steal, he will kill. So instead of just getting bogged down in one thing, Jesus looked at him and said, "Nicodemus, you must be born again."

He said, in other words, "Your whole structure must be changed." A nation that will keep people in slavery for 244 years will "thingify" them, make them things. Therefore they will exploit them, and poor people generally, economically. And a nation that will exploit economically will have to have foreign investments and everything else, and will have to use its military might to protect them. All of these problems are tied together. What I am saying today is that we must go from this convention and say, "America, you must be born again!"

So, I conclude by saying again today that we have a task and let us go out with a "divine dissatisfaction." Let us be dissatisfied until America will no longer have a high blood-pressure of creeds and an anemia of deeds. Let us be dissatisfied until the tragic walls that separate the outer city of wealth and comfort and the inner city of poverty and despair shall be crushed by the battering rams of the forces of justice. Let us be dissatisfied until those that live on the outskirts of hope are brought into the metropolis of daily security. Let us be dissatisfied until slums are cast into the junk heaps of history, and every family is living in a decent sanitary home. Let us be dissatisfied until the dark yesterdays of segregated schools will be transformed into bright tomorrows of quality, integrated education. Let us be dissatisfied until integration is not seen as a problem but as an opportunity to participate in the beauty of diversity. Let us be dissatisfied until men and women, however black they may be, will be judged on the basis of the content of their character and not on the basis of the color of their skin. Let us be dissatisfied. Let us be dissatisfied until every State capitol houses a Governor who will do justly, who will love mercy and who will walk humbly with his God. Let us be dissatisfied until from every city hall, justice will roll down like waters and righteousness like a mighty stream. Let us be dissatisfied until that day when the lion and the lamb shall lie down together, and every man will sit under his own vine and fig tree and none shall be afraid. Let us be dissatisfied. And men will recognize that out of one blood God made all men to dwell upon the face of the earth. Let us be dissatisfied until that day when nobody will shout "White Power!"—when nobody will shout "Black Power!"— but everybody will talk about God's power and human power.

I must confess, my friends, the road ahead will not always be smooth. There will still be rocky places of frustration and meandering points of bewilderment. There will be inevitable setbacks here and there. There will be those moments when the buoyancy of hope will be transformed into the fatigue of despair. Our dreams will sometimes be shattered and our ethereal hopes blasted. We may again with tear-drenched eyes have to stand before the bier of some courageous civil rights worker whose life will be snuffed out by the dastardly acts of bloodthirsty mobs. Difficult and painful as it is, we must walk on in the days ahead with an audacious faith in the future. And as we continue our charted course, we may gain consolation in the words so nobly left by that great black bard who was also a great freedom fighter of yesterday, James Weldon Johnson:

> Stony the road we trod,
> Bitter the chastening rod
> Felt in the days
> When hope unborn had died.

> Yet with a steady beat,
> Have not our weary feet
> Come to the place
> For which our fathers sighed?

> We have come over the way
> That with tears hath been watered.
> We have come treading our paths
> Through the blood of the slaughtered,

Out from the gloomy past,
Till now we stand at last
Where the bright gleam
Of our bright star is cast.

Let this affirmation be our ringing cry. It will give us the courage to face the uncertainties of the future. It will give our tired feet new strength as we continue our forward stride toward the city of freedom. When our days become dreary with low hovering clouds of despair, and when our nights become darker than a thousand midnights, let us remember that there is a creative force in this universe, working to pull down the gigantic mountains of evil, a power that is able to make a way out of no way and transform dark yesterdays into bright tomorrows. Let us realize the arc of the moral universe is long but it bends toward justice.

Let us realize that William Cullen Bryant is right: "Truth crushed to earth will rise again." Let us go out realizing that the Bible is right: "Be not deceived, God is not mocked. Whatsoever a man soweth, that shall he also reap." This is our hope for the future, and with this faith we will be able to sing in some not too distant tomorrow with a cosmic past tense, "We have overcome, we have overcome, deep in my heart, I did believe we would overcome."

## CHAPTER ELEVEN

## Black Power Bends Martin Luther King

Robert L. Scott

The Meredith March in Mississippi, June, 1966, occasioned
the confrontation of the slogans "Freedom Now" and "Black
Power." In his most recent book, Martin Luther King, Jr.,
presents a dramatic account of the struggle among the organizations that took over the march after James Meredith was
wounded by a shotgun blast. From the beginning, King testifies,
he sensed a tension, an antagonism to white participation in
the march, that he had not experienced during previous civil
rights actions. At Greenwood, Mississippi, "SNCC country,"
Stokely Carmichael brought the Black Power chant into the
open. Later at a conference of leaders to discuss the internal
tensions, and especially the new slogan, King reports:

> Stokely and Floyd [McKissick of CORE] remained
> adamant, and Stokely concluded by saying, with candor,
> "Martin, I deliberately decided to raise this issue on
> the march in order to give it a national forum, and force
> you to take a stand for Black Power."
> I laughed. "I have been used before," I said to Stokely.
> "One more time won't hurt."
> The meeting ended with the SCLC staff members still
> agreeing with me that the slogan was unfortunate and
> would only divert attention from the evils of Mississippi,
> while most CORE and SNCC staff members joined Stokely

SOURCE: This essay was first published in *Speaker and Gavel*, 5, 3 (March,
1968), 80–86. Reprinted by permission of the publisher, Delta Sigma Rho–Tau
Kappa Alpha.

and Floyd in insisting that it should be projected nationally. In a final attempt to maintain unity I suggested that we compromise by not chanting either "Black Power" or "Freedom Now" for the rest of the march.[1]

King's account of what occurred and his discussion of the significance of the slogan are credible. His book, appearing a year later, must have been written so close to the genesis of the debate that it can be considered part of the event, not later wishful thinking. Furthermore, King's public statements during and since the summer of 1966 are consistent with what he says in the book.

On one judgment few are likely to disagree with Dr. King. The effort to keep the internal controversy from distracting attention from the questions of civil rights in Mississippi was not successful. "But while the chant died out," King writes, "the press kept the debate going. News stories now centered, not on the injustices of Mississippi, but on the apparent ideological division in the civil rights movement."[2] Every newspaper and popular magazine had features on Black Power, usually with sides drawn pro and con from among civil rights organizations and leaders.[3] Martin Luther King was consistently presented as being against Black Power; that he symbolizes passive resistance helped translate the issue into violence versus non-violence. Anyone studying the evidence closely might question the propensity of the press to simplify the issue by enlisting King against Black Power, but no one can doubt that he was deeply troubled, and that while he was by no means as severe in his denunciations as was Roy Wilkins of the NAACP,[4] he believed the slogan would do more harm than good for the Negro.

---

[1] *Where Do We Go from Here: Chaos or Community?* New York, Harper & Row, Publishers, 1967, pp. 31–32.

[2] *Ibid.*, p. 32.

[3] See, for example, "Negro Leaders Dividing—The Effect," *U.S. News and World Report*, July 18, 1966, pp. 31–34.

[4] *Ibid.*, p. 34. Wilkins denounced the idea of Black Power vigorously in his address to the NAACP convention in Los Angeles. See *The New York Times*, July 6, 1966, p. 14, for excerpts.

Debaters, of course, seek to change the responses characteristic of their audiences. Participating in debate, however, may generate forces that will modify the participant as well. He may be brought to recognize limitations in his own position as he seeks to defend it against criticism. His recognition may stem both from arguments brought to bear by those who oppose him and from his own examination of his commitments as he finds himself pressing them on others. If he would appeal to an audience, the response tendencies which the debater must take into account will make the audience not merely a passive body to be shaped but an active force in shaping the discourse.

King's position on Black Power is an outgrowth of give and take with others within his own organization, the Southern Christian Leadership Conference—the parent of the Student Nonviolent Coordinating Committee, and with leaders of other organizations dedicated to civil rights; he has been pressed in scores of news conferences, radio and television programs, and public forums to denounce or defend Black Power. In such circumstances it is not surprising that Dr. King's voice has begun to sound some fresh notes.

In the decade following the Montgomery bus boycott, Martin Luther King became a symbol of passive resistance. Not only his ends but his means engendered controversy. Those who opposed equal rights for Negroes found his means difficult to resist. Peaceful demonstration and quiet practice of civil rights could only be countered by actions that dramatized the truth of the charges that King and his followers brought to bear. Those who stood for equal rights saw that King's means were consistent with his ends and honored him for setting an example of the strength of forbearance in the presence of evil.

King's methods have been important to him; he discussed them often, both inside "the movement" and with groups outside. To an organization of Presbyterian ministers and laymen called the Fellowship of the Concerned, he said in 1961,

> We cannot believe . . . the idea that the end justifies the means because the end is pre-existent in the means. So the idea of non-violent resistance . . . is the philosophy

which says that the means must be as pure as the end, that in the long run of history, immoral destructive means cannot bring about moral and constructive ends.[5]

In the sparsely furnished office of the man who was awarded the Nobel Peace Prize in 1964, a picture of Mohandas Gandhi testifies silently to King's indebtedness; he is not apt to forget his debt nor abandon the lesson he has striven so valiantly to teach others.

But King's ends and his means have been subjected to ridicule by the advocates of a new Negro militancy under the banner of Black Power.[6] "Freedom Now" has taken on a hollow ring in the face of token integration. The end of integration itself has been argued as suspect by Stokely Carmichael who pictures it as siphoning off a few of the most able Negroes from the black community leaving the many remaining the poorer for their absence.[7] Again, passive resistance, always difficult to practice, becomes more difficult as the militants remind Negroes that their passivity has always been praised as a virtue by white supremists: "We feel that integration is irrelevant; it is just a substitute for white supremacy. We have got to go after political power," Carmichael argues.[8] Some Negroes listened and at least applauded approval as H. Rap Brown went from city to city apparently fanning the fires of violence during the summer of 1967. "Stop looting and start shooting," newspapers reported him shouting to a crowd from atop a theater in riot-scarred Detroit. "The white man has declared war. We're in a rebellion."[9]

[5] "Love, Law and Civil Disobedience," in Roy L. Hill (ed.), *The Rhetoric of Racial Revolt*, Denver, The Golden Bell Press, 1964, p. 347.

[6] "At the CORE convention [July, 1966], middle-class Negroes were derided as 'black-power brokers,' 'handkerchief heads,' and 'Dr. Thomases' (Uncle Toms with attaché cases), and moderate Negro preachers like Dr. King were called 'chicken-eating preachers.'" Quoted from *Time*, July 15, 1966, p. 16.

[7] See, for example, "Toward Black Liberation," *Massachusetts Review*, **7**, 4 (Autumn, 1966), p. 647.

[8] Quoted in "SNCC Does Not Wish to Become a New Version of the White Man's Burden," *I. F. Stone's Weekly*, June 6, 1966, p. 3.

[9] Quoted in "Brown Presses Violence Theme," *Minneapolis Star*, Aug. 28, 1967, p. 6B.

The immediate impact of Black Power on Martin Luther King is not difficult to discern. Part of the "white backlash" was a dwindling of contributions to the civil rights movement.[10] Apparently anticipating the problem, in July, 1966, the SCLC sent a letter over Dr. King's signature to its list of supporters. It began, "This letter is not a fund appeal." King labeled the Black Power slogan as "an unwise choice at the outset" with "violent connotations" that have become injurious. After reaffirming his own and the SCLC's continued adherence to non-violence, he asserted that among the Negroes in Mississippi and Chicago with whom he had marched that summer "over 90% of these dedicated activists remained adherents of the time tested principles of non-violence and interracial unity." Most of the letter emphasized that conditions of racial inequality that spawned the frustration of violence continue.

In a letter over his signature in October, 1966, this time a fund appeal, Dr. King again disassociated himself and "the vast majority of Negroes" from Black Power (citing as evidence "a *Newsweek* poll" [August 22, 1966, p. 34]. But he subtly exploited the threat: "Yet it would be hazardous to be complacent or smug because the appeal of extremist Black Power is narrow. The allure of Black Power in its extremist or moderate senses springs from real, not imaginary causes." The letter pressed the miserable conditions to be dealt with, but with more emphasis on the urban ghetto than regular recipients of fund appeals from the SCLC had seen in the past. The readers were given implicit alternatives: accept the festering sores that lead to violence or support a constructive, non-violent organization. The letter concluded, "We need your support. Will you join with those who are investing in democracy? It will yield no profit except the satisfaction of shaping a future of brotherhood, freedom and harmony."

But the impact of Black Power on Martin Luther King has been more than that of immediate rhetorical necessities, such as disassociating himself from the violence, and of opportunities, such as presenting the SCLC as an alternative. In King

[10] See, for example, " 'A Major Turning Point' Against Negro Movement," *U.S. News and World Report*, Oct. 3, 1966, p. 46.

today there is more stress on building pragmatically economic and political strength and on using that strength, and there is a fresh emphasis on creating a sense of pride in Negro manhood. The change in direction was evident early in the furor over Black Power. A writer for *Newsweek* saw the turn taken: "Integration is out: The rallying cry for King's own campaign in Chicago is not 'integrate' but 'end slums'; the means, in effect, is Black Power without calling it that."[11]

In the year that followed the turbulent summer of 1966, Dr. King made pride and power consistent with love and non-violence. His new rhetoric is brilliantly displayed in his report to the Tenth Anniversary Convention of the Southern Christian Leadership Conference in Atlanta, Georgia, August 16, 1967.[12]

There is in this address, as one soon learns to expect in reading and listening to Dr. King, the repetitions of sound and phrase which give his speech a richly melodic quality. He begins by saying that Negroes a decade ago were "harried by day and haunted by night by a corroding sense of fear and a nagging sense of 'nobodyness.' " But pressure has caused "the sagging walls of segregation to come tumbling down" (p. 1). Throughout the opening, "ten years ago" is a refrain varied occasionally with "a decade ago." At the end of the speech, when King charges his hearers to keep their faith and renew their courage in the weary strife, "let us be dissatisfied" and finally "let us remember" and "let us realize" bring the drumbeat to his peroration (pp. 16–17).

But added to these familiar elements, to the allusions and direct references to the Bible, are echoes of the language of Black Power. Anyone who has heard and read Stokely Carmichael's angry words to white America, "I just want you to get off my back," may be jolted by King's "In short, over the last ten years, the Negro decided to straighten his back up, realizing that a man cannot ride your back unless it is bent" (p. 2). Even the black nationalism that has made common cause with revolutionaries around the world is reflected in

---

[11] July 11, 1966, p. 31.

[12] All references will be to the official version of the speech distributed by the SCLC, 334 Auburn Avenue, N.E., Atlanta, Ga.

King's "the ghetto is a domestic colony that's constantly drained without being replenished. You are always telling us to lift ourselves by our own bootstraps and yet we are being robbed every day. Put something back in the ghetto" (p. 6).

King's speech is a report on the past programs and future plans of the SCLC; it is also a refutation of the violent implications of Black Power, an absorption of the moderate implications of Black Power, and a challenge to a broadened task for those who have identified themselves with the civil rights movement. Underneath the subtle modifications of the language and the direct argument to these ends lies a well-wrought progression of thought in which each point prepares for the one that follows.

The speech opens appropriately with the stuff of a report. King uses the occasion of the tenth anniversary to stress past accomplishment, but the past accomplishment is focused to highlight a picture of radical change to cut some of the ground out from under the militants who have challenged King and his methods. "The courage with which [the Negro] confronted enraged mobs dissolved the stereotype of the grinning, submissive Uncle Tom. He came out of his struggle integrated only slightly in the external society, but powerfully integrated within. This was a victory that had to precede all other gains" (pp. 1–2).

Although the 1966 report had included the story of the SCLC's expansion into the northern ghettos with Operation Breadbasket, King's 1967 speech covers the work in Chicago and Cleveland in much more detail than that in the South. Such emphasis may be explained partially by recognizing that the delegates were more than well aware of the work in the South but needed to know more of the fresh accomplishments in the North, but even so, the stress on political and economic awareness and the molding of awareness into accomplishment occupies territory that the Black Power advocates saw as largely untouched by the drive for civil rights.

To the story of accomplishment and progress echoing with overtones of power, King adds another argument preparatory to a direct attack on Black Power. Picturing a nation in which the Negro's plight has been more than economic and political exploitation but one of psychological debasement. King calls upon the listener to "upset this cultural homicide," to affirm "his own Olympian manhood," to confirm "his psychological freedom" with "a firm sense of self-esteem." In doing so he adopts a phrase which had become associated with ghetto militants, "Yes, we must stand up and say, 'I'm black and I'm beautiful! . . .'" (p. 9).[13] King had often in the past appealed to self-esteem—his Christian sense of rightness set non-violence as the goal of a strong, dedicated man. But a pride in being black puts his drive for integration on a fresh basis, a little more like Stokely Carmichael's demand for a coalition of equal groups rather than an integration of selected individuals.

The lists of active accomplishments and the strong, proud identification with being black prepare the audience for the speaker's direct attack on violence. The first step in this attack is to define "legitimate power" as "the ability to achieve purpose" (p. 10); this step echoes the report of progress and promise just completed. The next step is to face the tension between "power" and "love":

> What is needed is a realization that power without love is reckless and abusive and love without power is senti-mental and anemic. Power at its best is love implementing the demands of justice, and justice at its best is power correcting everything that stands against love. And this is what we must see as we move on (p. 10).

The tension is resolved in Christian love. The failure to resolve the tension, to cry for the revenge of "destructive and con-scienceless power" is associated with the abhorrent reality of white supremacy (p. 11). This appeal is familiar to King's rhetoric: we must be better than they or sink even deeper to more shameful levels.

---

13 For an interesting account of Stokely Carmichael's use of "I am black and I am beautiful," in a speech in Tallahassee, Fla., Apr. 16, 1967, see Elizabeth F. Phifer and Dencil R. Taylor, "Carmichael in Tallahassee," *Southern Speech Journal*, **33**, 2 (Winter, 1967), p. 89.

After a thoroughly pragmatic attack on taking the idea of Black Power literally as revolution in America ("It is perfectly clear that a violent revolution on the part of American blacks would find no sympathy and support from the white population and very little from the majority of the Negroes themselves." p. 13), King proposes a deeper revolution: the restructuring of American society, which he relates to the confrontation of Jesus and Nicodemus, "America, you must be born again!" (p. 16).

King recognizes the pull that radical philosophy, economic and political, has had on many bright, young Negroes growing cynical in the contradictions of American life.

> What I'm saying to you this morning is that Communism forgets that life is individual. Capitalism forgets that life is social, and the Kingdom of Brotherhood is found neither in the thesis of Communism nor the antithesis of Capitalism but in a higher synthesis. . . . Now, when I say question the whole society, it means ultimately coming to see that the problem of racism, the problem of economic exploitation, and the problem of war are all tied together. These are the triple evils that are interrelated (p. 15).

Perhaps King never believed that his fight for integration was a fight to allow Negroes to be absorbed into a corrupt society, but his struggle with Black Power has made him emphasize the need for radical change. Whether this is an old or a new insight for King, he creates of it an opportunity to make a common cause with anyone, white or black, who will recognize that poverty, war, and hatred are symptoms of deep trouble that necessitate fundamental changes. Further he reaffirms his faith in non-violent methods on the familiar ground that violence will corrupt any change it brings.

Martin Luther King's address to the Tenth Anniversary Convention of the SCLC is an impressive document. In it the speaker displays a vocabulary freshened by its confrontation with Black Power and a program with more depth and breadth than the civil rights movement had known previously.

Of course no one, including Dr. King, can be certain of the influence of Black Power on his rhetoric. The SCLC had turned northward with Operation Breadbasket before the Meredith march; whether this drive would have assumed the importance it did in his 1967 report without the evident necessity of making some sort of response to Black Power is difficult to say. Further, Dr. King was disenchanted with the Vietnam war before the outcry of the well-known Black Power advocates.

In his 1966 report to the SCLC, Dr. King said, "But before we were able to depart from the 1965 Convention, the fires of Watts began to burn and with Watts a whole new era of the civil rights struggle emerged."[14] In this earlier presidential address, King touched on Black Power several times, but in 1967 direct and indirect references to the idea fascinating many Negroes permeates his report.

No one who reads or hears King can doubt that he is being influenced by a man who is rooted deeply in strong commitments, commitments which are not apt to be sundered in the changing winds of events. Nor can one doubt that here is a man who has exposed himself, and will expose himself, to the forces of change roaring about him. If indeed he has been bent in the debate over Black Power, bending may be a sign of strength; that which is bent may itself gain energy as a shaping force.

James Farmer, former director of CORE, writes that "the debate will rage on between cohesiveness and dispersion. Ascendancy of one camp or the other will be determined ultimately not by rhetoric, and not even by leadership, as much as by events. Events today seem to be racing to the side of the spirited new force—cohesion—and I think that is right and good for the black man at this historical juncture."[15] Farmer is right in seeing the priority of events in shaping the future and in judging that these are destined to arouse stronger feelings of

[14] "President's Annual Report by Dr. Martin Luther King, Jr., President, Southern Christian Leadership Conference, Delivered in Jackson, Mississippi, August 10, 1966." (Mimeographed, SCLC.)
[15] "Are White Liberals Obsolete in the Black Struggle?" *The Progressive,* January, 1968, p. 16.

community among Negroes. The question is on what terms will Negroes be cohesive? Would Farmer be able to identify the "spirited new force" at all if it were not in the process of developing some sort of recognizable character, which is about the same thing as saying if it were not being articulated by leaders.

If the next step forward for Negroes in America is to come through the development of organized political and economic power which will tend to emphasize the black community as a community, the problem of who will lead and with what philosophy is crucial. Writing in 1963, before the Black Power crisis, Martin Luther King saw the past failure of Negroes to shape and use power:

> Negroes have traditionally positioned themselves too far from the inner arena of political decision. Few other minority groups have maintained a political aloofness and a nonpartisan posture as rigidly and as long as Negroes. The Germans, Irish, Italians, and Jews, after a period of acclimatization, moved inside political formations and exercised influence. Negroes, partly by choice but substantially by exclusion, have operated outside of the political structures, functioning instead essentially as a pressure group with limited effect.[16]

The debate over Black Power has quickened King's concern for moving in directions he himself saw as necessary. Did he move soon enough? Is he moving quickly and substantially now? Does he judge the political acuity of his audience well: "By and large, Negroes remain essentially skeptical, issue-oriented, and independent-minded. Their lack of formal learning is no barrier when it comes to making intelligent choices among alternatives."[17] It is too early to answer these questions, but it is not too early to recognize that a man who has been predominant in the civil rights movement for the past decade

[16] *Why We Can't Wait*, New York, Harper & Row, Publishers, 1964, p. 163.
[17] *Ibid.*

is in the process of adapting his rhetoric to take advantage of and to modify the new force generated by an increasing awareness of the limitations of the old programs and a heady desire for exercising power as a group.

Martin Luther King, resilient and enduring, presents an insight and poses a challenge to all Americans. If America is to endure it must show itself capable of bending and shaping new ways in a new world. Some of our citizens have proved their capability to preserve and adapt in the most trying circumstances. In the rhetoric of Martin Luther King, all of us have much to heed and much to hope for.

## CHAPTER TWELVE

## An Advocate of Black Power Defines It

*Charles V. Hamilton*

"There is no Black Power movement singularly understood. There could hardly be," Charles V. Hamilton said in a speech at Hamline University (St. Paul, Minnesota, May 2, 1968). There are, rather, individuals and organizations which fall roughly into four categories.

"The political bargainer" conforms to established political processes. He can work within the two-party system comfortably. His principal interest is in equalizing opportunities to produce and obtain goods and services.

"The moral crusader" is less interested in goods and services than in what he is apt to refer to as the "soul of society." He is prone to mass demonstrations and stresses nonviolence. Since at some point along the route, he is apt to make agreements with the established power to gain goals from those who have not quite obviously been converted, he is open to the charges of "sell-out."

"The alienated reformer" is cynical about the possibilities of effecting change through existing structures. He stands hard for local control of black communities and demands equitable distribution of real decision-making power. A little like "the moral crusader," he hopes to transform society, but not through compassionate conversions, rather through gradual but substantial changes in the structure of the black community and its relationship to the larger society. Like "the political bargainer," he is interested in bread-and-butter issues, but he is contemptuous of "white middle-class values." He believes that there are worthwhile values to be learned by studying the history of black peoples and that a worthwhile value structure will emerge with the transformation of black communities.

"The alienated revolutionary" is also cynical about existing power structures. But he believes that change is unlikely to come except through calculated acts of instrumental violence. This sort of Black

SOURCE: This article is from *The New York Times Magazine* (Apr. 14, 1968), pp. 22–23, 79–83. Copyright © 1968 by The New York Times Company. Reprinted by permission of the copyright holders and the author.

Power advocate is apt to call for a separate black nation. He often begins as one of the other types and "is pushed by traumatic defeats" into the category of "alienated revolutionary," according to Hamilton.

Charles V. Hamilton brings to the Black Power controversy the training of the political scientist. He is a member of that faculty and chairman of the department at Roosevelt University in Chicago. He is coauthor with Stokely Carmichael of *Black Power: The Politics of Liberation in America.* He has spoken widely on Black Power and the article printed here shows the marks of his experience before audiences in developing his ideas. These ideas are those of a self-styled "alienated reformer."

Black Power has many definitions and connotations in the rhetoric of race relations today. To some people, it is synonymous with premeditated acts of violence to destroy the political and economic institutions of this country. Others equate Black Power with plans to rid the civil-rights movement of whites who have been in it for years. The concept is understood by many to mean hatred of and separation from whites; it is associated with calling whites "honkies" and with shouts of "Burn, baby, burn!" Some understand it to be the use of pressure-group tactics in the accepted tradition of the American political process. And still others say that Black Power must be seen first of all as an attempt to instill a sense of identity and pride in black people.

Ultimately, I suspect, we have to accept the fact that, in this highly charged atmosphere, it is virtually impossible to come up with a single definition satisfactory to all.

Even as some of us try to articulate our idea of Black Power and the way we relate to it and advocate it, we are categorized as "moderate" or "militant" or "reasonable" or "extremist." "I can accept your definition of Black Power," a listener will say to me. "But how does your position compare with what Stokely Carmichael said in Cuba or with what H. Rap Brown said in Cambridge, Md.?" Or, just as frequently, some young white New Left advocate will come up to me and proudly announce: "You're not radical enough. Watts, Newark, Detroit—that's what's happening, man! You're nothing but

a reformist. We've got to blow up this society. Read Ché or
Debray or Mao." All I can do is shrug and conclude that some
people believe that making a revolution in this country involves
rhetoric, Molotov cocktails and being under 30.

To have Black Power equated with calculated acts of violence would be very unfortunate. First, if black people have
learned anything over the years, it is that he who shouts revolution the loudest is one of the first to run when the action
starts. Second, open calls to violence are a sure way to have
one's ranks immediately infiltrated. Third—and this is as
important as any reason—violent revolution in this country
would fail; it would be met with the kind of repression used
in Sharpeville, South Africa, in 1960, when 67 Africans were
killed and 186 wounded during a demonstration against apartheid. It is clear that America is not above this. There are
many white bigots who would like nothing better than to
embark on a program of black genocide, even though the
imposition of such repressive measures would destroy civil
liberties for whites as well as for blacks. Some whites are so
panicky, irrational and filled with racial hatred that they would
welcome the opportunity to annihilate the black community.
This was clearly shown in the senseless murder of Dr. Martin
Luther King, Jr., which understandably—but nonetheless irrationally—prompted some black militants to advocate violent
retaliation. Such cries for revenge intensify racial fear and
animosity when the need—now more than ever—is to establish
solid, stable organizations and action programs.

Many whites will take comfort in these words of caution
against violence. But they should not. The truth is that the black
ghettos are going to continue to blow up out of sheer frustration and rage, and no amount of rhetoric from professors writing
articles in magazines (which most black people in the ghettos
do not read anyway) will affect that. There comes a point
beyond which people cannot be expected to endure prejudice,
oppression and deprivation, and they *will* explode.

Some of us can protect our positions by calling for "law
and order" during a riot, or by urging "peaceful" approaches,
but we should not be confident that we are being listened to

by black people legitimately fed up with intolerable conditions. If white America wants a solution to the violence in the ghettos by blacks, then let white America end the violence done to the ghettos by whites. We simply must come to understand that there can be no social order without social justice. "How long will the violence in the summers last?" another listener may ask. "How intransigent is white America?" is my answer. And the answer to that could be just more rhetoric or it could be a sincere response to legitimate demands.

Black Power must not be naive about the intentions of white decision-makers to yield anything without a struggle and a confrontation by organized power. Black people will gain only as much as they can win through their ability to organize independent bases of economic and political power— through boycotts, electoral activity, rent strikes, work stoppages, pressure-group bargaining. And it must be clear that whites will have to bargain with blacks or continue to fight them in the streets of the Detroits and the Newarks. Rather than being a call to violence, this is a clear recognition that the ghetto rebellions, in addition to producing the possibility of apartheid-type repression, have been functional in moving *some* whites to see that viable solutions must be sought.

Black Power is concerned with organizing the rage of black people and with putting new, hard questions and demands to white America. As we do this, white America's responses will be crucial to the questions of violence and viability. Black Power must (1) deal with the obviously growing alienation of black people and their distrust of the institutions of this society; (2) work to create new values and to build a new sense of community and of belonging; and (3) work to establish legitimate new institutions that make participants, not recipients, out of a people traditionally excluded from the fundamentally racist processes of this country. There is nothing glamorous about this; it involves persistence and hard, tedious, day-to-day work.

Black Power rejects the lessons of slavery and segregation that caused black people to look upon themselves with hatred and disdain. To be "integrated" it was necessary to deny one's heritage, one's own culture, to be ashamed of one's black skin, thick lips and kinky hair. In their book, "Racial Crisis in America," two Florida State University sociologists, Lewis M. Killian and Charles M. Grigg, wrote: "At the present time, integration as a solution to the race problem demands that the Negro foreswear his identity as a Negro. But for a lasting solution, the meaning of 'American' must lose its implicit racial modifier, 'white.' " The black man must change his demeaning conception of himself; he must develop a sense of pride and self-respect. Then, if integration comes, it will deal with people who are psychologically and mentally healthy, with people who have a sense of their history and of themselves as whole human beings.

In the process of creating these new values, Black Power will, its advocates hope, build a new sense of community among black people. It will try to forge a bond in the black community between those who have "made it" and those "on the bottom." It will bring an end to the internal back-biting and suspicious bickering, the squabbling over tactics and personalities so characteristic of the black community. If Black Power can produce this unity, that in itself will be revolutionary, for the black community and for the country.

Black Power recognizes that new forms of decision-making must be implemented in the black community. One purpose, clearly, is to overcome the alienation and distrust.

Let me deal with this specifically by looking at the situation in terms of "internal" and "external" ghetto problems and approaches. When I speak of internal problems, I refer to such things as exploitative merchants who invade the black communities, to absentee slumlords, to inferior schools and arbitrary law enforcement, to black people unable to develop their own independent economic and political bases. There are, of course, many problems facing black people which must be dealt with outside the ghettos: jobs, open occupancy, medical care, higher education.

The solution of the internal problems does not require the presence of massive numbers of whites marching arm in arm with blacks. Local all-black groups can organize boycotts of disreputable merchants and of those employers in the black communities who fail to hire and promote black people. Already, we see this approach spreading across the country with Operation Breadbasket, initiated by Dr. King's Southern Christian Leadership Conference. The national director of the program, the Rev. Jesse Jackson, who was with Dr. King when he was murdered in Memphis, has established several such projects from Los Angeles to Raleigh, N.C.

In Chicago alone, in 15 months, approximately 2,000 jobs worth more than $15 million in annual income were obtained for black people. Negotiations are conducted on hiring and upgrading black people, marketing the products of black manufacturers and suppliers and providing contracts to black companies. The operation relies heavily on the support of black businessmen, who are willing to work with Operation Breadbasket because it is mutually beneficial. They derive a profit and in turn contribute to the economic development of the black community.

This is Black Power in operation. But there is not nearly enough of this kind of work going on. In some instances, there is a lack of technical know-how coupled with a lack of adequate funds. These two defects constantly plague constructive pressure-group activity in the black communities.

CORE (Congress of Racial Equality) has developed a number of cooperatives around the country. In Opelousas, La., it has organized over 300 black farmers, growers of sweet potatoes, cabbages and okra, in the Grand-Marie Co-op. They sell their produce and some of the income goes back into the co-op as dues. Initially, 20 per cent of the cooperative's members were white farmers, but most of the whites dropped out as a result of social and economic pressures from the white community. An offshoot of the Grand-Marie group is the Southern Consumers' Cooperative in Lafayette, La., which makes and sells fruit cakes and candy. It has been in existence for more than a year, employs approximately 150 black people and has led to the formation of several credit unions and buying clubs.

The major effort of Black Power–oriented CORE is in the direction of economic development. Antoine Perot, program director of CORE, says: "One big need in the black community is to develop capital-producing instruments which create jobs. Otherwise, we are stuck with the one-crop commodity—labor—which does not produce wealth. Mere jobs are not enough. These will simply perpetuate black dependency."

Thus, small and medium-sized businesses are being developed in the black communities of Chicago, San Francisco, Detroit, Cleveland, New York and several other urban centers. CORE hopes to call on some successful black businessmen around the country as consultants, and it is optimistic that they will respond favorably with their know-how and, in some instances, their money. The goal is to free as many black people as possible from economic dependency on the white man. It has been this dependency in many places that has hampered effective independent political organizing.

In New York, Black Power, in the way we see it, operates through a group called N.E.G.R.O. (National Economic Growth and Reconstruction Organization). Its acronym does not sit too well with some advocates of black consciousness who see in the use of the term "Negro" an indication of less than sufficient racial pride. Started in 1964, the group deals with economic self-help for the black community: a hospital in Queens, a chemical corporation, a textile company and a construction company. N.E.G.R.O., with an annual payroll of $1 million and assets of $3 million, is headed by Dr. Thomas W. Matthew, a neurosurgeon who has been accused of failing to file Federal income-tax returns for 1961, 1962 and 1963. He has asserted that he will pay all the Government says he owes, but not until "my patient is cured or one of us dies." His patient is the black community, and the emphasis of his group is on aiding blacks and reducing reliance on the white man. The organization creates a sense of identity and cohesiveness that is painfully lacking in much of the black community.

In helping oneself and one's race through hard work, N.E.-G.R.O. would appear to be following the Puritan ethic of work and achievement: If you work hard, you will succeed. One gets the impression that the organization is not necessarily idealistic about this. It believes that black people will never develop in this country as long as they must depend on handouts from the white man. This is realism, whatever ethic it is identified with. And this, too, is Black Power in operation.

More frequently than not, projects will not use the term "Black Power," but that is hardly necessary. There is, for instance, the Poor People's Corporation, formed by a former S.N.C.C. (Student Nonviolent Coordinating Committee) worker, Jessie Norris, in August, 1965. It has set up 15 cooperatives in Mississippi, employing about 200 black people. The employees, all shareholders, make handbags, hats, dresses, quilts, dolls and other hand-craft items that are marketed through Liberty House in Jackson, Miss. Always sensitive to the development of the black community, the Poor People's Corporation passed a rule that only registered voters could work in the co-ops.

These enterprises are small; they do not threaten the economic structure of this society, but their members look upon them as vital for the development of the black people. Their purpose is to establish a modicum of economic self-sufficiency without focusing too much attention on the impact they will have on the American economic system.

Absolutely crucial to the development of Black Power is the black middle class. These are people with sorely needed skills. There has been a lot of discussion about where the black middle class stands in relation to Black Power. Some people adopt the view that most members of the class opt out of the race (or at least try to do so); they get good jobs, a nice home, two cars, and forget about the masses of blacks who have not "made it." This has been largely true. Many middle-class blacks simply do not feel an obligation to help the less fortunate members of their race.

There is, however, a growing awareness among black middle-class people of their role in the black revolution. On January 20, a small group of them (known, appropriately enough, as the Catalysts) called an all-day conference in a South Side Chicago church to discuss ways of linking black middle-class professionals with black people in the lower class. Present were about 370 people of all sorts: teachers, social workers, lawyers, accountants, three physicians, housewives, writers. They met in workshops to discuss ways of making their skills and positions relevant to the black society, and they held no press conferences. Though programs of action developed, the truth is that they remain the exception, not the rule, in the black middle class.

Another group has been formed by black teachers in Chicago, Detroit and New York, and plans are being made to expand. In Chicago, the organization is called the Association of Afro-American Educators. These are people who have traditionally been the strongest supporters of the status quo. Education is intended to develop people who will support the existing values of the society, and "Negro" teachers have been helping this process over the years. But now some of them (more than 250 met on February 12 in Chicago) are organizing and beginning to redefine, first, their role as black educators vis-à-vis the black revolution, and, second, the issues as they see them. Their motivation is outlined in the following statement:

"By tapping our vast resources of black intellectual expertise, we shall generate new ideas for *meaningful* educational programs, curricula and instructional materials which will contribute substantially toward raising the educational achievement of black children.

"Our purpose is to extricate ourselves momentarily from the dominant society in order to realign our priorities, to mobilize and to 'get ourselves together' to do what must be done by those best equipped to do it."

This is what they say; whether they can pull it off will depend initially on their ability to bring along their black colleagues, many of whom, admittedly, do not see the efficacy of such an attitude. Unless the link is made between the black middle-class professionals and the black masses, Black Power will probably die on the speaker's platform.

Another important phenomenon in the development of Black Power is the burgeoning of black students' groups on college campuses across the country. I have visited 17 such campuses—from Harvard to Virginia to Wisconsin to U.C.L.A.—since October. The students are discussing problems of identity, of relevant curricula at their universities, of ways of helping their people when they graduate. Clearly, one sees in these hundreds (the figure could be in the thousands) of black students a little bit of Booker T. Washington (self-help and the dignity of common labor) and a lot of W. E. B. DuBois (vigorous insistence on equality and the liberal education of the most talented black men).

These are the people who are planning to implement social, political and economic Black Power in their home towns. They will run for public office, aware that Richard Hatcher started from a political base in the black community. He would not be Mayor of Gary, Ind., today if he had not first mobilized the black voters. Some people point out that he had to have white support. This is true; in many instances such support is necessary, but internal unity is necessary first.

This brings us to a consideration of the external problems of the black community. It is clear that black people will need the help of whites at many places along the line. There simply are not sufficient economic resources—actual or potential—in the black community for a total, unilateral, boot-strap operation. Why should there be? Black people have been the target of deliberate denial for centuries, and racist America has done its job well. This is a serious problem that must be faced by Black Power advocates. On the one hand, they recognize the need to be independent of "the white power structure." And on the other, they must frequently turn to that structure for help—technical and financial. Thus, the rhetoric and the reality often clash.

Resolution probably lies in the realization by white America that it is in her interest not to have a weak, dependent, alienated black community inhabiting the inner cities and blowing them up periodically. Society needs stability, and as long as there is a sizable powerless, restless group within it which considers the society illegitimate, stability is not possible. However it is calculated, the situation calls for a black-white rapprochement, which may well come only through additional confrontations and crises. More frequently than not, the self-interest of the dominant society is not clearly perceived until the brink is reached.

There are many ways whites can relate to this phenomenon. First, they must recognize that blacks are going to insist on an equitable distribution of *decision-making power*. Anything less will simply be perpetuating a welfare mentality among blacks. And if the society thinks only in terms of *giving* more jobs, better schools and more housing, the result will be the creation of more black recipients still dependent on whites.

The equitable distribution of power must result from a conviction that it is a matter of mutual self-interest, not from the feelings of guilt and altruism that were evident at the National Conference of New Politics convention in Chicago in August. An equitable distribution means that black men will have to occupy positions of political power in precincts, counties, Congressional districts and cities where their numbers and organization warrant. It means the end of absentee white ward committeemen and precinct captains in Chicago's black precincts.

But this situation is much easier described than achieved. Black Americans generally are no more likely to vote independently than other Americans. In many Northern urban areas, especially, the job of wooing the black vote away from the Democratic party is gigantic. The established machine has the resources: patronage, tradition, apathy. In some instances the change will take a catalytic event—a major racial incident, a dramatic black candidate, a serious boner by the white establishment (such as splitting the white vote). The mere call to "blackness" simply is not enough, even where the numbers are right.

In addition, many of the problems facing black people can be solved only to the extent that whites are willing to see such imperatives as an open housing market and an expanding job market. White groups must continue to bring as much pressure as possible on local and national decision-makers to adopt sound policy in these fields. These enlightened whites *will* be able to work with Black Power groups.

There are many things which flow from this orientation to Black Power. It is not necessary that blacks create parallel agencies—political or economic—in all fields and places. In some areas, it is possible to work within, say, the two-party system. Richard Hatcher did so in Gary, but he first had to organize black voters to fight the Democratic machine in the primary.

The same is true of Mayor Carl Stokes in Cleveland. At some point it may be wise to work with the existing agencies, but this must be done only from a base of independent, not subordinated, power.

On the other hand, dealing with a racist organization like George Wallace's Democratic party in Alabama would require forming an independent group. The same is true with some labor unions, especially in the South, which still practice discrimination despite the condemnation of such a policy by their parent unions. Many union locals are willing to work with their black members on such matters as wages and working conditions, but refuse to join the fight for open housing laws.

The point is that black people must become much more pragmatic in their approach. Whether we try to work within or outside a particular agency should depend entirely on a hard-nosed, calculated examination of potential success in each situation—a careful analysis of cost and benefit. Thus, when we negotiate the test will be: How will black people, not some political machine downtown or some labor union boss across town, benefit from this?

Black Power must insist that the institutions in the black community be led by and, wherever possible, staffed by blacks. This is advisable psychologically, and it is necessary as a challenge to the myth that black people are incapable of leadership. Admittedly, this violates the principle of egalitarianism ("We hire on the basis of merit alone, not color"). What black and white America must understand is that egalitarianism is just a *principle* and it implies a notion of "color-blindness" which is deceptive. It must be clear by now that any society which has been color-conscious all its life to the detriment of a particular group cannot simply become color-blind and expect that group to compete on equal terms.

Black Power clearly recognizes the need to perpetuate color consciousness, but in a positive way—to improve a group, not to subject it. When principles like egalitarianism have been so flagrantly violated for so long, it does not make sense to think that the victim of that violation can be equipped to benefit from opportunities simply upon their pronouncement. Obviously, some positive form of special treatment must be used to overcome centuries of negative special treatment.

This has been the argument of the Nation of Islam (the so-called Black Muslims) for years; it has also been the position of the National Urban League since its proposal for preferential treatment (the Domestic Marshall Plan, which urged a "special effort to overcome serious disabilities resulting from historic handicaps") was issued at its 1963 Denver convention. This is not racism. It is not intended to penalize or subordinate another group; its goal is the positive uplift of a deliberately repressed group. Thus, when some Black Power advocates call for the appointment of black people to head community-action poverty programs and to serve as school principals, they have in mind the deliberate projection of blacks into positions of leadership. This is important to give other black people a feeling of ability to achieve, if nothing else. And it is especially important for young black children.

An example of concentrated special treatment is the plan some of us are proposing for a new approach to education in some of the black ghettos. It goes beyond the decentralization plans in the Bundy Report; it goes beyond the community involvement at I. S. 201 in Harlem. It attempts to build on the idea proposed by Harlem CORE last year for an independent Board of Education for Harlem.

Harlem CORE and the New York Urban League saw the Bundy Report as a "step toward creating a structure which would bring meaningful education to the children of New York." CORE, led by Roy Innis, suggested an autonomous Harlem school system, chartered by the State Legislature and responsible to the state. "It will be run by an elected school board and an appointed administrator, as most school boards are," CORE said. "The elected members will be Harlem residents. It is important that much of the detailed planning and structure be the work of the Harlem community." Funds would come from city, state and Federal governments and from private sources. In describing the long-range goal of the proposal, CORE says: "Some have felt it is to create a permanently separate educational system.

Others have felt it is a necessary step toward eventual integration. In any case, the ultimate outcome of this plan will be to make it possible for Harlem to choose."

Some of us propose that education in the black community should be family-oriented, not simply child-oriented. In many of the vast urban black ghettos (which will not be desegregated in the foreseeable future) the school should become the focal point of the community. This we call the Family-Community-School-Comprehensive Plan. School would cease to be a 9-to-3, September-to-June, time-off-for-good-behavior institution. It would involve education and training for the entire family—all year round, day and evening. Black parents would be intimately involved as students, decision-makers, teachers. This is much more than a revised notion of adult education courses in the evening or the use of mothers as teachers' aides.

This plan would make the educational system the center of community life. We could have community health clinics and recreational programs built into the educational system. Above all, we could re-orient the demeaning public welfare system, which sends caseworkers to "investigate" families. Why could we not funnel public assistance through the community educational program?

One major advantage would be the elimination of some of the bureaucratic chaos in which five to ten governmental agencies zero in on the black family on welfare, seldom if ever coordinating their programs. The welfare department, for one, while it would not need to be altered in other parts of the state, would have to work jointly with the educational system in the black community. This would obviously require administrative reorganization, which would not necessarily reduce bureaucracy but would consolidate and centralize it. In addition to being "investigators," for example, some caseworkers (with substantially reduced case loads) could become teachers of budgetary management, and family health consultants could report the economic needs of the family.

The teachers for such a system would be specially trained in a program similar to the National Teacher Corps, and recruits could include professionals as well as mothers who could teach classes in child-rearing, home economics, art, music or any number of skills they obviously possess. Unemployed fathers could learn new skills or teach the ones they know. The curriculum would be both academic and vocational, and it would contain courses in the culture and history of black people. The school would belong to the community. It would be a union of children, parents, teachers, social workers, psychologists, urban planners, doctors, community organizers. It would become a major vehicle for fashioning a sense of pride and group identity.

I see no reason why the local law-enforcement agency could not be integrated into this system. Perhaps this could take the form of training "community service officers," or junior policemen, as suggested in the report of the President's Commission on Civil Disorders. Or the local police precinct could be based in the school, working with the people on such things as crime prevention, first aid and the training of police officers. In this way, mutual trust could be developed between the black community and the police.

Coordinating these programs would present problems to be worked out on the basis of the community involved, the agencies involved and the size of the system. It seems quite obvious that in innovations of this sort there will be a tremendous amount of chaos and uncertainty and there will be mistakes. This is understandable; it is the price to be paid for social change under circumstances of widespread alienation and deprivation. The recent furor about the Malcolm X memorial program at I.S. 201 in Harlem offers an example of the kind of problem to be anticipated. Rather than worrying about what one person said from a stage at a particular meeting, the authorities should be concerned about how the Board of Education will cooperate to transfer power to the community school board. When the transfer is made, confusion regarding lines of authority and program and curriculum content can be reduced.

The longer the delay in making the transfer, however, the greater the likelihood of disruption. One can expect misunderstanding, great differences of opinion and a relatively low return on efforts at the beginning of such new programs. New standards of evaluation are being set, and the experimental concept developed at I.S. 201 should not be jeopardized by isolated incidents. It would be surprising if everything went smoothly from the outset.

Some programs *will* flounder, some will collapse out of sheer incompetence and faulty conception, but this presents an opportunity to build on mistakes. The precise details of the Comprehensive Plan would have to be worked out in conjunction with each community and agency involved. But the *idea* is seriously proposed. We must begin to think in entirely new terms of citizen involvement and decision-making.

Black Power has been accused of emphasizing decentralization, of overlooking the obvious trend toward consolidation. This is not true with the kind of Black Power described here, which is ultimately not separatist or isolationist. Some Black Power advocates are aware that this country is simultaneously experiencing centralization and decentralization. As the Federal Government becomes more involved (and it must) in the lives of people, it is imperative that we broaden the base of citizen participation. It will be the new forms, new agencies and structures developed by Black Power that will link these centralizing and decentralizing trends.

Black Power structures at the local level will activate people, instill faith (not alienation) and provide a habit of organization and a consciousness of ability. Alienation will be overcome and trust in society restored. It will be through these local agencies that the centralized forces will operate, not through insensitive, unresponsive city halls. Billions of dollars will be needed each year, and these funds must be provided through a more direct route from their sources to the people.

Black Power is a developmental process; it cannot be an end in itself. To the extent that black Americans can organize, and to the extent that white Americans can keep from panicking and begin to respond rationally to the demands of that organization —to that extent can we get on with the protracted business of creating not just law and order but a free and open society.

## CHAPTER THIRTEEN

## The Rhetoric of Black Power: Order and Disorder in the Future

*Robert L. Scott and Wayne Brockriede*

In the voice of Black Power rings a militant symbolic justification of violence which both terrifies and challenges blacks and whites. But also the voice suggests a redemptive power— the social and economic power to transform the individual and the society in which he lives. Part of the rhetorical power of the term lies in its ambiguity. Even those made fearful must admire the virtuosity with which the Black Power advocate plays out his role and the dynamic quality of that role in the contemporary scene.

We are reminded of the madman about whom Plato makes Socrates speak in the *Gorgias*—a madman stalking through a crowd with a dagger up his sleeve. He has tyrannical power; but Socrates cannot respect this power since it is that that any madman might have. We notice, however, that our situation is more complex. We are faced with advocates referring to madmen, suggesting that the daggers may be up their sleeves—and with good reason in a mad society, asking what it is about that society that drives men mad, and wondering what crowd could be worse. Does this mob deserve to live?

The degree to which Black Power advocacy is responsible for the great outbursts of violence in our cities is hotly argued; the Riot Commission's report suggests that such advocacy is no important part of the cause. The degree to which Black Power advocacy has been responsible for great outbursts of self and societal analysis is readily apparent. Whatever Black Power is or does, it undeniably implies some new ideas and strikes a new interpersonal stance.

Black Power implies three ideas: an emphasis on black pride and on the black person's right to define and to structure the terms in which the struggle for racial equality is to be waged; a reinterpretation of integration as a need to assimilate black communities *as groups* into the larger society rather than to siphon off able black people, one by one, into that society; and a generally more militant insistence that ghetto conditions be improved now, an insistence which makes its point partially by being willing to step across the line of nonviolence into violence.

The new stance of Black Power denies the appropriateness of the role of the black suppliant, the black person, hat in hand, asking the great white father to confer new benefits. Black Power advocates repudiate a society in which power is located overwhelmingly among white people, exercised through channels almost exclusively white. They consider the Civil Rights Acts of 1964 and 1965 "gifts" from white to black (seen as "generous" by whites but as "tokens" by blacks). The rhetoric of Black Power assumes that such a societal structure is not likely to yield genuine gains and that suppliance by black people is not only predictably ineffective but unbecoming. The new stance asserts interpersonal parity. Black people are to recognize that blackness is beautiful, that they need not deny their racial identity or integrity to gain political and economic power, that they must organize their communities to revolutionize the power structure rather than to continue ineffectual attempts to tinker with it.

These new ideas communicated from this new stance constitute a declaration of war. Whether that war is to be a symbolic cold war or a violent revolution will be determined largely by the response to the rhetoric of Black Power.

The response so far has not been encouraging. It varies between eager backlash and sorrowful disassociation. One dominant reaction has been to insist on law and order: Policemen should imprison spokesmen, shoot arsonists, and maim looters. Some of the people with this reaction were restrained by Martin Luther King's nonviolent rhetoric by recognizing that white violence against black nonviolence would unleash sympathies which might alter the status quo. These people now gleefully escalate the real violence of the ghettos and the symbolic violence of Black Power.

A second reaction is to insist on law and order but to do so through the massive deployment of manpower and through curfews rather than through unrestrained firepower. This reaction shares with the first a determination to maintain the status quo and to stop the riots; it differs only in the method of control.

A third reaction is to freeze civil rights and antipoverty legislation, to refuse to "bend the knee" to the Negro's violent demands until he "behaves himself" and thereby earns special consideration.

A fourth reaction is to advocate a concession or two to head off militance and violence. The Open Housing bill of 1968 seems to fall into this category.

All four responses presuppose white superiority and will not achieve a peace or even a truce. The cold war will grow hotter, summer by summer. Some people propose a different kind of response. The President's Commission on Civil Disorders, Bayard Rustin, Whitney Young, Nelson Rockefeller, and others advocate a domestic Marshall Plan of truly gigantic proportions: the spending of over a hundred billion dollars over the next ten or twelve years to create housing and jobs.

Perhaps most significant about these similar recommendations is that they come from men who have long been associated with moderate politics. The rhetorical significance of this fact is brilliantly underscored in Tom Wicker's introduction to the report of the Commission on Civil Disorders:

> But just as it sometimes takes a Hawk to settle a war— Eisenhower in Korea, De Gaulle in Algeria—so did it take bona fide moderates to validate the case that had to be made. A commission made up of militants, or even influenced by them, could not conceivably have spoken with a voice so effective, so sure to be heard in white, moderate, responsible America. And the importance of this report is that it makes plain that white, moderate, responsible America is where the trouble lies.[1]

Militants may not have been present; but surely the militant voice was heard in the report. It echoes in Mr. Wicker's sentences,

[1] *Report of the National Advisory Commission on Civil Disorders*, New York, Bantam Books, Inc., 1968, p. v.

giving a biting irony especially to the use of the word "responsible."

A domestic Marshall Plan has several significant advantages. To a black person, fooled for so long by promises not kept and by programs pitifully small, the very size of the proposal has symbolic appeal. One hundred billion dollars is no token. The very size of the expenditure might convince a black person that the white man was finally committed, pocketbook and all, to the proposition that the disparity of white and black economic conditions must end.

But this proposal misses a significant feature of Black Power rhetoric. That rhetoric contends that black people must develop their own power to take what is rightfully theirs: a full opportunity to achieve full political and economic equality with white people. The Black Power advocate does not want a handout, however massive, from a benevolent, superior white liberal. If the proposal is a gift from white to black, administered by white people (with the participation of an appropriately integrated Negro or two) in an effort to help the black person *rise* into white society, it will not work. Such a conception might have been accepted in the early years of the 1960s, but it will be rejected now.

What, then, is a response to the rhetoric of Black Power which offers some hope for a just reconciliation? Massive and judicious expenditures of money are necessary but not sufficient. A second condition is the clarification that what is appropriated is not a gift but a restoration of rights long denied. Third, white men must recognize the legitimacy of preserving black identity and must not assume that a black man has worth only when he permits himself to be assimilated into white society. Fourth, black communities must have the political power to participate actively in determining the policy and in spending the money to improve their economies. This final condition could be met by something like neighborhood development corporations. Prototypes of such organizations are now being evolved around the country. They are neither governmental nor private corporations, although both elements are involved. The resulting mixtures give the participating citizens opportunities to determine what their own needs are and how these will be met. Through such units some urban citi-

198 The Rhetoric of Black Power

zens are taking a hand in running health centers, schools of various sorts, and even business enterprises. Perhaps most important, financing, which is not simply self-perpetuating handouts, is being made available cheaply enough to be utilized. Whether or not such programs will be massive enough and work soon enough remains to be seen. But if successful, they may do more than help set right some long overdue social debts. They may evolve patterns for community relationships essential for a decent urban life in a rapidly evolving technocracy. New ways of adjusting self to community and community to self are desperately needed in twentieth-century America, and not just by blacks. Someday, perhaps, the sort of thought apparent in Martin Luther King's last presidential address to the Southern Christian Leadership Conference or in Charles V. Hamilton's essay for *The New York Times Magazine* may be seen as prefiguring significant structural changes in American urban life.

In the future, Black Power attacks on the larger society will hold more hope if the response to them begins to exploit the positive values present. Such responses may lead a large portion of the white majority to see the possibility not merely of striking uneasy truces but of truly transforming their own living conditions.

The immediate future of race relations in this country will be affected not only by the continuing rhetoric of Black Power and by the rhetorical response of white society, but by the rhetoric of such groups as the Southern Christian Leadership Conference. Black Power prodded Martin Luther King and his group to modify their position and to alter their interpersonal rhetoric. King had followed Carmichael in stressing black pride and in focusing on the economic conditions of the ghettos. He had become more than ever determined to achieve racial justice. But King's rhetoric differed from Carmichael's on two counts: (1) He tried to identify the interests of blacks and whites and to cooperate with white leadership. (2) He was unalterably opposed to violence. In the early months of 1968 he planned a Poor People's March to Washington. This was to be his response to the rhetoric of Black Power: a rhetoric of identification, of nonviolence, but of militance.

Would it work? Several factors predicted it would not. Non-violence had lost some of its appeal for those impatient with recent failures of that method to stir the Establishment from its apathy. On the other hand, King's increased militance annoyed white liberals who thought that the time was not right to press for domestic expenditures in the wake of increased costs in Vietnam and the President's request for a tax increase. The extent to which poor white people would join the march, moreover, was problematic.

But a somewhat more optimistic view was possible, too. Some people hoped desperately that a middle position could be found between the polarized extremes of Black Power and White Backlash. In addition, Nobel Prize winner Martin Luther King still symbolized the civil rights movement, still possessed enormous charismatic power, and still had a large following. If the rhetorical thrust of a Poor People's March to Washington could work, the precisely right man was its leader.

On April 4, 1968, in Memphis, Martin Luther King, Jr., was assassinated. The militant nonviolent group had lost its leader. The national mourning which followed was second in recent years only to that in 1963 for John F. Kennedy. King's death, like Kennedy's, required the ritual performance of grief; only a few Americans in public life abstained from participation.

The death of Martin Luther King raises two questions, and with these we conclude our examination of the rhetoric of Black Power. First, would King, like Kennedy, leave memorials of legislation? The Open Housing bill, thought to be in serious congressional trouble, passed quickly after the assassination. But many persons, ourselves included, regarded this law as close to tokenism. The more serious concerns of King, the guaranteed annual income and other large-scale antipoverty measures, appear doomed. Some of the Presidential candidates apparently favor parts of the program, but no one of them gives such advocacy primary emphasis.

What of the memorial of the Poor People's March? The SCLC has continued plans which their leader had initiated. The march will occur. The message of the march will not inhere in numbers, as in 1963, but in the determination and endurance of those who participate. But Washington officials are apprehensive, more antagonistic than supportive. Although Martin Luther King had secured an agreement from Stokely Carmichael not to oppose the march and to offer some support, Black Power advocates do not appear to be involved enthusiastically in the project. The common prediction is that somehow violence will result from the march.

The second question is one of leadership. Very soon after the assassination, commentators assumed that Rev. Ralph Abernathy would be the new leader of the SCLC. The assumption proved accurate. Could Abernathy lead effectively?

He had two immediate tasks: to function rhetorically in the rites of mourning and to complete the coordination of the Poor People's March. He performed admirably the first task in moving speeches in Memphis and Atlanta. The second he is in the process of conducting as we conclude this book. He seems to be making appropriate rhetorical decisions. His language and his behavior seem not much different from Dr. King's. Abernathy has a flair for the phrase, and he projects determination, as in a speech in Atlanta:

> The bill for generations of irresponsibility, oppression, and neglect is being presented for payment. It is long overdue. The bill is going to be collected—willingly or unwillingly, in civilized human decency and love, or in fear and hate and the flames of destruction. Time is not running out, but rather, time has run out.[2]

At this time, of course, Abernathy does not have the charismatic power of King, but he may well have the potentiality for developing it.

The concept of charisma is difficult to pin down. Some men appear to have power which binds others to them and to a cause. Sociologist Edward Shils believes that charisma springs from fundamental order. All men, he argues, have a need for some sort of order which gives to their experiences meaningful rela-

[2] The May 8, 1968, speech was reported in an Associated Press dispatch of that date.

tionships; all men, therefore, attribute respect to some ordering principles and to institutions which embody or men who symbolize them. On the other hand:

> Order-destroying power, great capacity for violence, attracts too, and arouses the charismatic propensity. It does so because it promises in some instance, to provide a new and better order, one more harmonious with the more inclusive and deeper order of existence. Order-destroying power also arouses the charismatic propensity because of a profound ambivalence in man's relations to the central things. Order not only gives meaning; it also constricts and derogates. . . . Great power announces itself by its power over order; it discovers order, creates order, maintains it, or destroys it. Power is indeed the central, order-related event.[3]

To those who have glimpsed potential sources of new power in America and have tasted its bittersweet flavor, we would echo the words of Nietzsche's Zarathustra. "There is nobody from whom I want beauty as much as from you who are powerful: let your kindness be your final self-conquest. Of all evil I deem you capable: therefore I want the good from you. Verily, I have often laughed at the weaklings who thought themselves good because they had no claws." The Black Panther has claws; but its beauty will lie with its truth and the effectiveness of its truth with its rhetoric.

Black Power seeks racial equality by developing the political and economic and symbolic power of the black community to take it, violently if need be. Ralph Abernathy's Poor People's Power seeks the same goal by exhibiting nonviolently at least a similar degree of commitment by poor people of all races. The central questions in May, 1968, are these: How shall they develop their rhetorical strategies? How shall white America respond?

[3] "Charisma, Order, and Status," *American Sociological Review*, **30**, 2 (April, 1965), pp. 204–205.

# A Postscript to the Reader: A Few Words About Criticism

A rhetorical perspective is a way of looking at how men use symbolic behavior to influence other men and events. This conception implies three primary dimensions which critics must consider.[1]

First, rhetoric is a transaction among people. The rhetorician makes many interpersonal decisions. Who should address whom? Which audiences should be treated as primary? How compatible with a speaker are these potential listeners? Should he aim at identification with them or alienation? Should he be relatively personal or relatively impersonal? Should he try to relate to his audiences as a hero, an agent, a peer, or a suppliant? How credible is he to his audience?

Second, rhetoric is a transaction of ideas. The rhetorician also makes ideational decisions. What philosophical positions does he take? What ideology is he to represent? How should he define his terms? What policies should he advocate? What attitudes and values should he employ as premises? What social norms should he invoke? What data should he use? How should he structure his discourse? What style should he develop as consistent with all his other decisions?

Third, rhetorical transactions occur in unique situations.[2] The rhetorician decides how to structure the way he and others per-

---

[1] These dimensions are developed more thoroughly in Wayne Brockriede, "Dimensions of the Concept of Rhetoric," *Quarterly Journal of Speech*, **54**, 1 (February, 1968), pp. 1–12.

[2] An interesting recent characterization and emphasis of the situational dimension is Lloyd F. Bitzer, "The Rhetorical Situation," *Philosophy and Rhetoric*, **1**, 1 (January, 1968), pp. 1–14.

ceive the situation. What functions does the situation invite or prescribe? What formats should he employ in it? What channels are appropriate to it? To what social contexts should he relate the situation?

The rhetorical perspective involves a complex set of interacting dimensions, any combination of which may produce insights into the nature and probable consequences of the rhetorical act or process. It is not a collection of formulas rigidly to be applied. Rather, it is a way of looking at a transaction. The critic is most likely to find something of value if he looks closely at an act from the points of view of whatever dimensions seem to reward the scrutiny.

In this volume we have criticized the rhetoric of Black Power generally and the discourses of Hubert Humphrey, Stokely Carmichael, and Martin Luther King in particular. We are immodest enough to hope that you have learned something of Black Power and of the rhetorical perspective.

But we have a second purpose. We invite you to make your own criticism of the rhetoric of Black Power. Your criticism will shape your future reactions to the rhetoric that plays an important part in the evolving patterns of racial relations in America. Your criticism may even take forms intended to evoke responses from others. In any case, we suggest specifically that you criticize two sorts of discourse.

First, criticize criticism. Our own criticism of the rhetoric of Black Power represents only one point of view. As you look at somewhat different materials relating to these events, giving them different dimensions and drawing from a background of different experiences and ideas, you will see things we did not see. You will learn more about Black Power and about rhetoric.

One thing you might learn is that criticism is potentially multipurposed. The critic seeks to understand the object of his interest, but in doing so he throws into bold relief the value structure from which he works. Criticism is always an exercise in self-awareness and is perhaps that of the strongest sort since it does not contemplate in isolation but demands self-knowledge in relation to other human beings and human products.

You may learn further that critical effort is not necessarily something which is set apart from the forces that give rise to aesthetic objects. It can be a part of the force that creates fresh situations and a part of the force that creates a taste and an ability to work with zest in rapidly evolving symbolic transactions.

We offer no formulas, no preconceived standards, no outline of categories to help you in your task. We suggest only that you learn a great deal about the speaker, the audience, their interpersonal and ideational interaction together, the issues of the controversy, and the situational context; that you approach your task with a great deal of critical curiosity and with a spirit of inquiry; and that you mix together your knowledge and your inquiry.

Second, criticize the Black Power movement as it develops further. What is the quality of the decisions which Stokely Carmichael, H. Rap Brown, Floyd McKissick, and others will make in communicating themselves and their ideas to their audiences, black and white—militant, moderate, and conservative? What kind of interpersonal stance will they take toward their various audiences? What ideas will they emphasize? What situations and channels will they utilize? What changes in style will they develop?

What is the quality of the response to that rhetoric which others will make? Will white liberals continue to disassociate themselves from militant Black Power? Will they show a greater understanding of the rationale for justifying violence—even though they may not approve of violence? Will they recognize why Black Power advocates are impatient with tokenism and with white power supremacy? Will they continue to deplore the divisiveness of "black racism"? Or will they cooperate in the formation of a new coalition of equals with the black community toward the establishment of economic and political parity?

Can the followers of Martin Luther King forge a rhetoric which can transcend Black Power and synthesize black and white, moderate and militant? What role will Ralph Abernathy play toward such mediation? Can Abernathy and others maintain nonviolence while stressing a determination not to be turned around as they march for their rightful place in the American Dream?

Will some third force come into being which is neither the old civil rights movement nor the militant black reaction? Are we now hearing fresh notes sounded by men like Dick Gregory and Nathan Wright, Jr.? What sort of effect will the election of Negro mayors in Gary, Indiana, and Cleveland, Ohio, as well as what is certain to be an increasing trend of the election and appointment of black officials throughout the nation, have on the atmosphere in which all future confrontations of apathy and anger, pride and fear will take place?

Can some group or individual develop a rhetorical strategy that will cause whites and blacks to unite on common goals? Can a new idea or a new kind of human relationship create an effective rhetoric for racial justice and equality? Must Black Power continue its strident note of alienation and revolution before society at large listens? Must the system be burned down?

These and other questions may be relevant as men continue to write and speak on issues of Black Power. Your criticism of these discourses will give you a better understanding of Black Power and of the rhetorical perspective. Each of us must take final responsibility for forming a coherent view of the vital questions living poses for us. On the basis of our views, we must be ready to interact with others if we are to make any sort of contribution to a decent human community.

## Suggested Readings

Many readers will want to read further on the issue of Black Power. Few will have any difficulty finding material, but we shall list a few books and magazine articles that we found especially interesting.

### Books

Breitman, George (ed.): *Malcolm X Speaks*, New York, Grove Press, Inc., 1966.

Carmichael, Stokely, and Charles V. Hamilton: *Black Power: The Politics of Liberation in America*, New York, Random House, Inc., 1967.

Essien-Udom, Essien Udosem: *Black Nationalism: The Search for an Identity*, Chicago, University of Chicago Press, 1962.

Fager, Charles E.: *White Reflections on Black Power*, Grand Rapids, Mich., William Eerdmans, 1967.

Fanon, Frantz: *The Wretched of the Earth*, trans. by Constance Farrington, New York, Grove Press, Inc., 1963.

Hill, Roy L. (ed.): *The Rhetoric of Racial Revolt*, Denver, The Golden Bell Press, 1964.

King, Jr., Martin Luther: *Where Do We Go from Here: Chaos or Community*, New York, Harper & Row, Publishers, 1967.

King, Jr., Martin Luther: *Why We Can't Wait*, New York, Harper & Row, Publishers, 1964.

Wright, Jr., Nathan: *Black Power and Urban Unrest: Creative Possibilities*, New York, Hawthorne Books, Inc., 1967.

Wright, Richard: *White Man, Listen!* Garden City, N. Y., Doubleday and Co., 1957.

### Articles

Bennett, Jr., Lerone: "Stokely Carmichael: Architect of Black Power," *Ebony*, September, 1966, pp. 25–32.

Burgess, Parke G.: "The Rhetoric of Black Power: A Moral Demand?" *Quarterly Journal of Speech*, **54**, 2 (April 1968), 122–133.

Danzig, David: "In Defense of 'Black Power,' " *Commentary*, September, 1966, pp. 41–46.

Detweiler, Bruce: "A Time to Be Black," *New Republic*, Sept. 17, 1966, pp. 19–22.

Farmer, James: "Are White Liberals Obsolete in the Black Struggle?" *Progressive*, January, 1968, pp. 13–16.

Good, Paul: "A White Look at Black Power," *The Nation*, Aug. 8, 1966, pp. 112–117.

Mack, Raymond W.: "The Negro Opposition to Black Extremism," *Saturday Review*, May 4, 1968, pp. 52–55.

Millspaugh, Frank: "Black Power," *Commonweal*, Aug. 5, 1966, pp. 500–503.

Phifer, Elizabeth Flory, and Dencil R. Taylor: "Carmichael in Tallahassee," *Southern Speech Journal*, 33, 2 (Winter 1967), 88–92.

Roberts, Gene, "The Story of Snick: From 'Freedom High' to 'Black Power,' " *The New York Times Magazine*, Sept. 25, 1966, pp. 27–29; 119–128.

Rustin, Bayard: " 'Black Power' and Coalition Politics," *Commentary*, September, 1966, pp. 35–40.

Warren, Robert Penn: "Two for SNCC," *Commentary*, April, 1965, pp. 38–48.

Weinraub, Bernard: "The Brilliancy of Black," *Esquire*, January, 1967, pp. 130–135.

Wheeler, Harvey, "A Moral Equivalent for Riots," *Saturday Review*, May 11, 1968, pp. 19–22, 51.